Michael]
POCKET
SALTWAT]

C000153307

Michael Prichard started writing in the ....
school of Fleet Street, and having acquired the
skills of the journalist he left for quieter waters.
As a fishing tackle adviser, he travels far and
wide in the pursuit of good tackle design. He
has directed a number of angling films, and has
broadcast regularly on radio and TV.

With a life-long fascination with fishing in all
its forms, Mike has sought every species of
interest to the sportfisherman and succeeded in
taking many fine specimens from freshwater
and saltwater. His prowess with the camera
(he is an Associate of the Royal Photographic
Society) enables him to publish first-class evidence of his catches. In 1978 and 1979 Mike
captained England at international sea fishing
festivals in Connemara and Youghal, Republic
of Ireland, and in both years his team beat
strong opposition from the rest of the British
and Continental teams. For many years he also
organized the popular Guinness sea angling
contests in Dingle, Republic of Ireland.

A desire to pass on his wide knowledge of the
sport has led to the encouragement and instruc-
tion of young anglers in many areas of Britain.
Among the author's books are his *Pocket Guide
to Freshwater Fishing*, *Pocket Guide to Bait and
Lures*, *Pocket Guide to Spinning* (the com-
panions to this book), the best-selling *Encyclo-
pedia of Fishing in Britain and Ireland*, and
Fishing for Beginners, all published by Collins.

COMPANION BOOKS

Michael Prichard's Pocket Guide to Freshwater Fishing
Michael Prichard's Pocket Guide to Bait and Lures
Michael Prichard's Pocket Guide to Spinning

Michael Prichard's
POCKET GUIDE TO
SALTWATER FISHING

Collins

Published by William Collins Sons & Co. Ltd.
London and Glasgow.
Text, photographs and diagrams © Michael Prichard 1982
Fish profile paintings © William Collins Sons & Co. Ltd. 1977, 1982
First published 1982
Reprinted with revisions 1985 and 1987

Printed and bound in Great Britain by
William Collins Sons & Co. Ltd.

ISBN 0 00 411646 1

CONTENTS

INTRODUCTION

Sea angling is the fastest growing branch of the sport of fishing. Throughout Western Europe, there are men and women, living a long way from the sea, who accept the challenge of the elements to lure the denizens of the deep. Throughout the year, they travel to the sea for its excitement, mystery and its sporting fish. This is a book about the how and why of sea fishing. The techniques are those that I have proven over many years of happy, successful sea angling. Many of the methods discussed were handed down to me, their origins lost in the history of past angling exploits. Some have come to me as a result of a poor day or a tiresome wait, when wind and weather combined to keep me ashore.

We have much to learn about the oceans and those incredible animals that live in this rigorous environment. It is one sporting situation where the quarry exists in a habitat that is completely alien to our own. The hunter or wildfowler, if he is a patient and intelligent observer, comes to know much of the lifestyle of his beast or bird. We anglers cannot be among the fish to accompany them on their fantastic oceanic migrations, though it is the observant, thinking angler who enjoys the bulk of catches and success. Fishing is a thing of the mind, its value to the individual extremely difficult to describe. What I have tried to achieve within these pages is give you a brief explanation of the fish, their way of life and the simple methods that have evolved since our sport began. (*Freshwater Fishing*, the companion title to this book, covers coarse and game fishing.)

Sea angling has two distinct divisions among its followers: those that fish from boats; and an army of anglers that patrol the lonely shoreline. The species may differ but the thrill of single-handed combat is the same. There are no seasons other than those dictated by the movements of the fish. The North Atlantic weather will determine who leaves his warm fireside and how many of the sport's followers will wait for the softer days of spring and summer. But to each of us, sea angling spells a freedom from the everyday cares of office and workshop. In this volume I want to take you fishing in saltwater for those marine species that haunt the littoral waters of the British Isles and the seaboard of north and western Europe.

Michael Prichard, ARPS

Two of the ocean's predators: the fighting, ever-hungry tope and its captor, well-known sea angler Jim McLanaghan, of Scotland.

(Above) *The build-up of inshore sandbanks and bars is a continual process. Gravel and silt are carried down from highland, heath and farmland. This material serves to fertilize the littoral zone.*
(Below) *The fishing zones for shore anglers and boat fishermen.*

The fishing zones

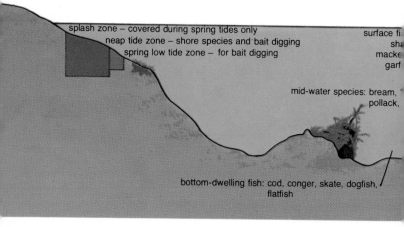

splash zone – covered during spring tides only
neap tide zone – shore species and bait digging
spring low tide zone – for bait digging

surface fi
sha
macke
garf

mid-water species: bream,
pollack,

bottom-dwelling fish: cod, conger, skate, dogfish,
flatfish

THE SEA AND ITS FISHING

The sea is the richest source of protein on this planet. Unlike the land mass, which is only fertile on its surface, the waters of our seas have the potential of providing a rich food source in depth. Protein, both in the form of fish and plankton, can be reaped from the pelagic layers as well as the demersal deeps. For our sport we fish in comparatively shallow waters. Fishing beyond the 50 fathom (90 m) mark becomes a gruelling exercise. But luckily most of the European angling species live and breed in the shallow waters of the Continental Shelf. On average, the Continental Shelf extends for a distance of 10–15 miles (16–24 km) from the shores of Western Europe. We acknowledge a depth of about 100 fathoms (180 m) as being the edge of this Shelf. Beyond that point we have the Continental Slope leading down to the Abyss where the depths reach down to over 2,000 fathoms (3,500 m).

The British Isles are particularly fortunate in having a large area of the Shelf around their coasts. The whole of the North Sea lies on the Shelf. This is because the area of the North Sea was formerly a land connection to Europe lying in shallow water. Our rivers have spewed silt and minerals from the land to create further shelves. The Continental Shelf is widest where the land rose up when the seawater levels dropped and is narrowest where there were areas of land upheaval, perhaps due to subterranean activity, and movement caused by the Ice Ages.

Fish and other forms of marine life live on or over the Continental Shelf because it is a fertile plain constantly enriched by minerals washed from the land mass. Vegetation grows abundantly down to below 30 fathoms (55 m), with 60 fathoms (110 m) possibly the maximum depth at which rooted plants can grow. The sea is not rich in plant variety when compared with the mass of plantlife that covers the earth. There are very few flowering plants in the sea other than those of the splash zone. Most of the vegetation is composed of simple algae. There are many drifting plant forms, most of which are minute, that make up the phyto-plankton which forms a valuable food for minute invertebrates and fish fry.

Sea angling is comparatively new as a sport. It really began in the last part of the nineteenth century when people augmented the contents of the family larder by handlining. The rod and line then gave an extension to the thrill of catching fish. This sporting tackle also enabled man to land a larger fish on lighter line than would have been possible with a handline.

There are many different marine habitats around our shores and out

9

in the deeper water offshore. Fish species have widely varied requirements which need to be present in an area before they will take up residence. Some fish live over a sandy seabed as they feed on animals that live there. These fish can also disguise their presence, either by burrowing under the top layers of sand or by having bodies displaying colour patterns that create a near-perfect camouflage. Naturally, these fish have a sandy-brown colour. The rocky shore is a place offering security and an abundance of creatures that live attached to the rocks. Weed growth cuts down light penetration so that the environment is dark in some areas and brightly light in others. Fish that live here often have bodies magnificently and brightly coloured, so matching their surroundings. The predators, like the pollack, are dark greenish-black on the back and silvery-green on the belly. This gives them the advantage of being camouflaged from above and below as their body colouring matches the dark of the ground and the brilliance of the sky.

Fish that live on mixed ground display similar colouring, sometimes covered with spots and marbled markings that blend into the all-over colour pattern of the habitat. At some period in their lives most marine fish migrate from one habitat to another. The migration may be seasonal for breeding or feeding purposes and can cover journeys of thousands of miles. The blue fin tunny, a fish that used to be caught in the North Sea before World War II, has been tagged in the Carribean before beginning its annual migration across the Atlantic Ocean. Tunny have been caught bearing tags indicating that the fish had swum almost to the northern coast of Norway. Similarly, black bream come to the undersea chalk cliffs off Littlehampton, off the Sussex coast, every year. They travel from Mediterranean waters to breed there each May.

There are marine species that feed throughout the year in saltwater but must enter our rivers to spawn. The salmon is a fish that feeds in the deep Atlantic yet breeds in the headwaters of many European rivers. The freshwater eel and conger leave our rivers and offshore rocky areas to migrate once in their lifetime. Both species are thought to travel to spawn in the tropical Sargasso Sea—a calm area in the North Atlantic, between the West Indies and the Azores, where there is an abundance of floating seaweed of the genus *Sargassum*. Where fish travel to is of interest to us, as anglers, because much of our angling expertise depends on waylaying them on the outward journey and upon their return. Fish keep to a rigid timetable during their migrations and anglers are aware of this. It is by knowing the individual species' needs of food, habitat and migration that we are able to catch them regularly. So take my advice, learn fish behaviour and become a better angler.

(Right) *Bluefin tunny are among the world's finest gamefish. This large specimen was caught off the prolific fishing area at Gran Canaria, where these fish are found in very large numbers at certain times of the year. The Canaries, Spanish islands off the north-west coast of Africa, attract many sea anglers for bluefin, bonito, large blue shark, marlin, yellowfin and bigeye tuna, mako shark and broadbill tuna, thresher shark and wahoo.* (Below) *The well-known sea vegetation forms that fringe the shoreline: there is kelp, also known as Poor Man's Weather Glass, bladder wrack and other brown and green seaweeds.*

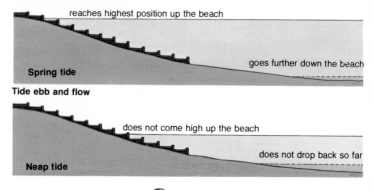

reaches highest position up the beach

goes further down the beach

Spring tide

Tide ebb and flow

does not come high up the beach

does not drop back so far

Neap tide

What causes the tides

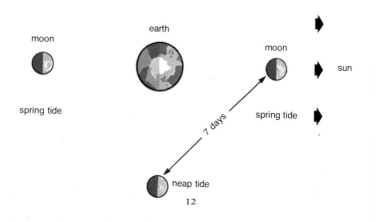

moon

earth

moon

sun

spring tide

spring tide

7 days

neap tide

SEA ANGLING ENVIRONMENTS

The shingle shore

Shingle beaches are formed by the constant movement of tide that rolls pieces of fallen cliff along the seabed. Huge boulders are ground into polished pebbles that make up the famous banks. At first sight, it may be difficult to understand why many shingle beaches produce good fishing. Pebble banks are infertile, there is little life to be found within the piles of shingle. To find the fish-holding areas we must look beyond the shingle bank, out to where strong currents have scoured channels in the sand. The shingle is only a clue to the kind of tidal action that we can expect—strong water that forces small fish into a situation where they become prey for the larger, stronger fish. The same strong currents will wash all manner of invertebrate life into a stream of feed particles that are gathered in certain places. Dungeness Point and its famous 'Dustbin' is a case in point, where the prevailing currents have built up a massive shingle projection that diverts the tide but creates a larder of food for fish. Some shingle beaches have great length instead of jutting out into the sea. Chesil beach along the Dorset coast and Shingle Street, an East Anglian winter cod mark, have currents that sweep along the shingle, piling the pebbles up to create high banks. The gradient is continued underwater, for off these shingle shores the water is quite deep close inshore and the bottom is relatively clean. There can be little weed growth, nor can encrusting creatures be found for there is little for them to adhere to. Worms are the main food source for the fish, which usually means that the shingle beach is cod country, although whiting and other species will appear at some time in the angler's year.

(Top left) *A heaped pebble shore at Shingle Street, Suffolk.*
(Centre left) *Rise and fall of the tides.* (Left) *The gravitational pull of the sun and moon creates the tides.* (Right) *On a shingle beach, low tides often expose a flat, sandy seabed beyond the shingle where fish move in to search for marine creatures as food. This area cannot be seen at high tide so the angler must memorise its layout.*

The sandy shore

The sandy beach may be composed of pure, golden sand above the low-water mark, but under the water the seabed is often made up of a mixture of sand, mud and silt. This type of ground is populated by worms, both the lugworm and ragworm, with a number of burrowing molluscs. These are chiefly of the bivalve species that can move about, on or among the top layers of sand, using a foot that protrudes from the double shell housing the animal. Cockles, clams and razorfish form a major part of the diet of the fish that feed over the shallow areas of the sandy strands. There will be scant weed and no musselbeds there because, as with the shingle beach, there is no firm base for the weed to root in or the sedentary shellfish to adhere to. Occasionally there will be outcrops where the undersand bedrock rises above the level of the seabed. Here, rock-dwelling shellfish and some of the lesser seaweeds will take a hold. These areas form miniature rocky habitats that attract a few crustaceans to hide within the security of the rocky crannies. Small shore crabs, squat lobsters and tiny fish species such as gobies and blennies also appear. The worms are there in profusion: both the rag and lugworm form baitbeds in the inter-tidal zone. This is a perfect fishing habitat, for the feed potential encourages a wide variety of different fish to work across the open ground.

14

(Left) *A storm beach, composed of shallow, clean sand over which the surf rolls.* (Right) *A sandy bay with rock spurs at each end offers two quite different fishing areas.* (Below) *Useful fishing here: rocky outcrops project out to a clean sand seabed, with weedy patches giving a home for many creatures that fish feed on. But take care when rock fishing.*

Sand-reef situations

There are many places around the shores of the British Isles, Norway and, to some extent, the coast of south-west France, where sandy beaches are fringed at either end by a rocky outcrop to form a bay. The rocks usually extend as a reef spur that juts out into the sea at right angles to the coastline. These are reefs of hard rock that the tidal action cannot erode as fast as it does the softer shales and sandstones. So they become breakwaters, natural obstructions to the lateral tide action throughout much of the tidal phase. This leaves a gentle seabed where minute animals can live without being constantly scoured out of the sand. The reefs do two things for the sea angler: they provide a natural pier to walk out onto, giving him access to the slightly deeper water, *and* a perfect habitat for fish to exist in. The reef walls give security in a multitude of hiding places. Food is available from animals living on the rock faces and the creatures that venture out onto the clean sand between the rocky spurs. This varied environment, with its deeper water offered by the reefs, demands varying angling styles. To the normal legered bait-casting we can now add the art of spinning. The addition of another

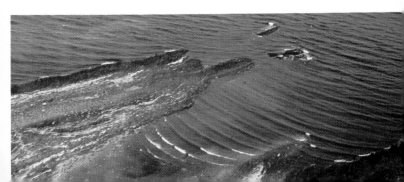

habitat factor means that there are more species likely to patrol the improved feeding grounds. Float fishing too begins to enter our thoughts, providing the water is deep enough to harbour the wrasse and pollack, these species providing good float-fishing sport.

The rocky shoreline

This habitat can be the most productive of all the shore angler's environments. The ground can be clean sand, a mixture of sand and small rocks, or pure rock—and pure hell—for the fisherman's tackle. But the fact is that where we lose tackle is where fish are likely to be! Deep water close under your rod will give the best fishing, as it ensures a resident population of fish species as well as providing a suitable holding area for those fish that move in to feed. Deep water will mean wrasse during the warmer months, pollack when there are fry about and the usual species that scavenge along the jungle of kelps that grow in this kind of habitat. Big fish, the superior predatory species like tope and porbeagle shark, do venture into the rock fisherman's domain if there is sufficient depth to give them confidence. The large predators probably need both a food availability and a strong feeling of security before they swim close to the cliff faces. Most of the renowned rock fishing marks are in the west and south-west stretches of the European coast line. They are therefore washed by warmer waters which gives a quicker growing shellfish population and a larger resident fish community.

The rocky shore introduces an extension of the fishing area. Unlike the open beaches, where fish are to be found taking food from the bottom, the rocky habitat gives fish feeding areas throughout the depths. There will be sub-surface feeders such as mackerel and pollack; mid-

water fish, like the rock codling, wrasse and inshore ling; and other species that scavenge at the base of the cliffs and among the boulders that form the seabed. Skates and rays, conger eels, specimen bass, and larger specimens of many species will be found over this ground.

Piers, breakwaters and harbour walls

These environments are capable of offering boat fishing without the angler actually being at sea. Any man-made projection out into deepwater will attract both vegetation and minor marine creatures. A food source becomes well established that draws fish like a magnet. The form of construction used in harbours and piers, where stone blocks are laid in courses, provides a vast area of cracks and crevices that provide homes for fish. Because of the proximity of human habitation, it is inevitable that edible rubbish will find its way into the water. Among the detritus will be food particles that fish come to expect. If the harbour is a working one containing a few commercial fishing vessels, there will be fish oil, scales and flesh finding its way into the harbour. Conger particularly roam the areas alongside a fish quay. Summertime will mean the arrival of shoals of mullet, another fish that scavenges around the fishing trawlers and pleasure yachts. This feeding behaviour can be used to advantage by sea anglers. We can simulate the small fish particles by making up mixtures of mashed fish, oil and bread. Fed down from the harbour walls, this groundbait will wash around in the water to be discovered by resident fish. Gradually they become accustomed to the feed and the human activity on the harbour wall above their heads. A hookbait introduced among the 'browse' will soon be accepted by mullet, but stealth is the secret of success.

(Left) *This rocky shore has a number of underwater hazards. Flat ledges make ideal fishing platforms. Float-fishing will avoid the continual snagging that would occur with the legering techniques.* (Right) *A pier constructed from piles of loose rocks. It is below the water for half of the tidal phase. Weed and attached shell-fish and crustaceans create a source of food to bring fish within angling range.*

Estuaries

The last of our shore fishing habitats can be divided into two clearly defined types. The first is the short river that enters the sea through a narrow outlet with good depth of water. Many of the West Country, Scottish and Irish spate rivers, as well as the fjords of Scandinavia, have an estuary of this conformation. Secondly, we have the broad, shallow river mouths that have many channels and banks of silt. Both forms of estuary can provide fine fishing but the approach to the angling and the methods differ. The deep, narrow river mouth often indicates a river that flows down through high country. Speed of flow and the rocky make-up of the land mass give us clean water with little suspended sediment. There is a lush weed growth with a profusion of encrusting shellfish on the coastline and piers of landing stages. This habitat is perfect for float fishing and spinning close-in. The deep channel gives us baitcasting for the demersal species that move into the river on each tide. Here there is an over-riding flow of freshwater on to the rich saline tidal press which can bring some freshwater species into the estuary mouth. Slob trout will often be found above flounders and bass.

The wide, muddy estuary has a gentle flow of freshwater that almost

stands still when the oncoming tide pushes into the river. These estuaries are most often found where a broad river meanders through agricultural land, bringing a heavy stream of earth particles. The water is dirty and there is a continual build-up of mudbanks with gouging of channels to take away the land water at low tide. Slow-flowing freshwater and shallow depths mean that the two kinds of water are more readily mixed, so the marine species found in this environment are those that can tolerate brackish water. Flounders, mullet and scavenging bass feed over the algae on the mudflats although only the flounders and mullet will remain throughout the tidal phase. Such a river-estuary creates a fertile river mouth as the nutrient content of the land water is high. Unfortunately there are often heavy industrial uses of the river bank, so we can expect an element of man-made pollution. With reasonable cleanliness, the estuarine waters will support shrimp and prawn, with myriads of tiny creatures such as shore crabs, all of which form a large part of the fish's diet. If there is a problem in fishing this kind of water it is that shallow ground, riddled with deep-cut channels, spells danger to the unwary angler when the tide rushes in, covering the hazards. Water-and-mud-filled waders are anchors!

(Top left) *Mullet, possibly the most wary and difficult sea fish to catch, melt away into the shadows at the first sign of any unusual activity. The angler must avoid sudden movements that create vibrations.* (Left) *Estuaries are fertile, food-growing areas producing vegetable and animal life that constitute food for fishes.* (Above) *The mud flats of the typical estuary are cut into channels which meander across them, nearly emptying at low tide. As the tides come in, hungry flounder, bass and mullet follow up to feed on the creatures that live in the rich mud, and knowing anglers are ready and waiting for them!*

In assessing all of the shore fisherman's environments, the most important thing to do is to become totally familiar with the varied habitats. The angler must visit the fishing ground at the bottom of low-water spring tides when all of his potential fishing area is uncovered. Only then can any angler see what he has to cope with in terms of underwater obstructions, channels, reefs and clean ground. There are very good reasons why fish take up residence or visit a place to feed. These creatures are instinctively aware that they require a given amount of feed each day to satisfy their appetites. This feeding behaviour may mean that the fish develop a pattern of migration from one area to another that we anglers can come to learn. Then ambush becomes possible!

Deepsea over clean ground

Fish are not spread evenly over the seabed waiting for us to arrive with baited hooks. They are constantly on the move feeding or avoiding predators. Clean ground, meaning a bottom made up of sand, mud or a mixture of both, can be absolutely flat and featureless. But there will

Lining up an inshore mark

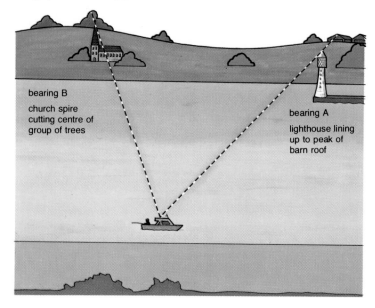

bearing B

church spire cutting centre of group of trees

bearing A

lighthouse lining up to peak of barn roof

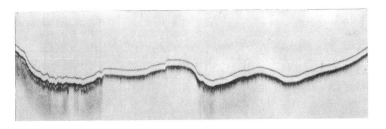

(Above) *An echo-sounder trace taken while the craft was moving over fairly flat, sandy ground. On the 30 ft (10 m) scale, the area shown here is about 100 yd (91 m), compressing undulations of the seabed.* (Below left) *Accurate cross-bearings, to locate a known fishing mark, depend on lining up prominent objects to be seen on the shore. If the four objects in bearings A and B are in line from the boat, the craft is on the known mark.*

always be subtle features that cause fish to linger or perhaps live for definite periods in the year. Sand and mud are a perfect medium for burrowing shellfish and marine worms to live in. Providing the sea angler knows where these feeding grounds are, fishing can be effective throughout the year as one species after another moves across our offshore grounds. This is a knowledge that successful charter skippers acquire. Taking sea angling parties out day after day gives the party boat-owner the opportunity to have many rods out on a greater number of days than could be managed by the dinghy fisherman. There aren't many sea anglers who can get to sea more than twice a week but there are many ways of building and storing angling knowledge. By taking and recording accurate marks, from cross bearings to shoreline buildings or navigation buoys, skippers can ensure re-location of a particular patch of productive ground. Open ground fishing is always difficult. The establishment of defined marks depends on so many factors including natural feed availability, state of tide, weather and time of year.

Deepsea over sandbanks

This is a clean-ground situation that isn't difficult to find. Sandbanks are a natural obstruction to tide flow and a hazard to the navigation of all vessels. So they are marked by buoys, lightships and channel hazard markers in heavily used areas. A sandbank is constantly on the move, being changed in location and size by the power of the sea. Some banks have tops that rise above the surface at all stages of the tide whereas others can only be found by their navigational warning signs or on an

Admiralty chart. They can all provide suitable fish-holding habitats. Some small species, like the sandeel, will live in the bank, burrowing down into the sand when strong tides make the going tough. Other fish—cod, tope and turbot—take up station around the bank where conditions of water flow give them an advantage over the smaller fish. The predators are able to grab them as the current sweeps them away from the security of the bank. Around the base of the sandbank there will be a natural scour where the strongest current flow runs around the sand's bulk. In this channel the feed is concentrated, so the larger specimens gather for the harvest to be brought to them. Here is where the angler's bait ought to be, but anchoring above such a place can be a hazardous operation, not to be undertaken by the novice. The turbot is one of the species that feeds on the bank. They lie on the downtide side, just over the lip of the bank where sandeels and fry are brought to them on the flowing tide. So you see that to fish the bank efficiently positioning the boat is critical and must be slightly adjusted as the tide varies in both direction and strength. At times of slack water or on weak neap tides, the sandbanks can be fished from a drifting boat. Of course, the boat must be continually motored uptide after each drift but this can be a satisfying, all-action sea angling technique.

Deepsea over mixed ground

A mixture of sand, mud, shingle and rocks forming the bed of the sea gives the angler a wide variety of habitat *and* species. With its greater variation in the constituents of the seabed, nature has provided more feed availability and living conditions. The roughness of the bottom creates something to which marine plants can attach themselves. Each fold in the rock, each jagged crevice or plant stem becomes a home for a marine animal, somewhere that is protected from the continual battering from prevailing currents or heavy swell reaching down to the seabed in times of heavy weather. Unlike open-ground areas, where fish have to depart into deeper water when the inshore seas are in turmoil, the rough ground always provides an element of shelter, so the fish are ever present. An increase in species and population gives more food possibilities to predators. Dogfish, skates and rays and bottom-dwelling congers become available to rod and line. The rougher the ground the less chance there is that trawlers will be able to clean the seabed. Trawling methods, especially with modern equipment involving the use of heavy otterboards and bobbins, cause an even greater worry. Their actions can destroy the habitat by disturbing the make-up of the bottom ground. Clam raking and the 'ploughing-out' methods used when shellfishing are even more destructive as they smash shellbeds up.

Deepsea over rock and reef

This kind of fishing mark demands accuracy in one's angling approach. We need to fish alongside outcrops of rock and undersea reefs to catch most of the species that dwell there. Over the top of the mark we *do* find fish, although they are normally the smaller species that prefer clear water from where they can see the approach of possible danger. There is evidence of a vertical migration during the dark hours of some of the larger species. Both pollack and conger are known to rise almost to the

A very different echo-sounder trace from that shown on page 21.
Here, the boat is positioned over a fish-bearing pinnacled reef.

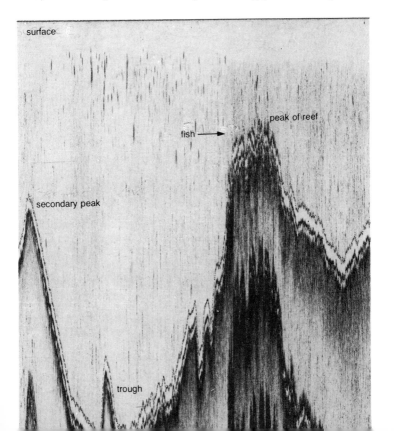

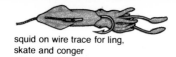

squid on wire trace for ling, skate and conger

6 ft/2 m

sandeel, on sink-and-draw rig, for pollack

prawn for bass

(Left) *Natural baits that will draw fish from pinnacled reefs: squid, sandeel and shrimp. Care must be taken not to snag the hooks on the weed and rocks on the face of the reef.* (Right) *The cliffs of Moher, Co Clare. Beneath these spectacular and steep buttresses are found the fabulous porbeagle fishing grounds that have made this wild Atlantic mark famous. A little farther south, many porbeagle have been caught by Irishman Jack Shine while fishing off the rocks.*

surface late in the evening and into the night. This seems to be a summertime phenomenon, probably connected with the fact that there will be shoals of fry around at that time of the year.

It is the mid-water section of a reef that gives the best fishing opportunities. Ling, pollack, coalfish, cod and many other species abound. They live and feed at different levels that can be plotted quite accurately. To get to the fish we have to position the boat very carefully. The bait needs to be lowered so that it drops past close to the rock face. Reef-dwelling species come out from holes in the rock to the attack so, with the constant predator-prey relationship, all fish have to grab a bait and then dive for their lair. The reef will support a big population of fish around its base, fish that rely on food coming from above their heads. This will be either carcases that sink down as a result of natural mortality, or mortal wounding from an attack higher up the rocky buttress. Down here live the slow-moving scavengers, conger and skates, with occasional visits from tope and other shark species. Large fish, with the porbeagle shark the frequent example, will elect to remain cruising the periphery of a reef for long periods. They feed heavily on mackerel when the shoals come in but depend on the pollack for their round-the-year diet. Where there is a powerful tidal flow, places like the Scottish offshore islands and Irish Atlantic peninsulas, the halibut appears. This is the largest of the flatfishes and is a live-fish feeder that chooses to hang in the tide, just out of the strongest flow, from where it drives at pollack and other roundfish.

The reef environments are hard on an angler's tackle, the seabed around being littered with broken lines and lost leads. But this must be the acme of deepsea ground fishing. Where tackle is lost is where the best fish always are. Reef fishing demands accuracy in positioning the boat together with a simple, efficient tackle method that is the key to success over the pinnacles.

(Above) *The moment of supreme compression, when a beach-casting rod is put to the greatest test. Long-distance casting from the shore is perhaps the most demanding skill of all angling techniques.*

TACKLE FOR SHOREFISHING

There are three basic forms of shorefishing. By far the most popular system must be casting out natural baits—worms and so on—to lie on the bottom as a legered offering. All but the pelagic shoal species, of which mackerel are the most important, will take these baits. The tackle styles can be varied to suit conditions of both seabed make-up and tide. So all but the roughest of broken ground can be bottom fished. Fish of the upper water layers—mackerel, garfish, mullet and small pollack—provide the float fisherman with his sport. This angling method will also cope with fishing situations where the seabed is far too rough for a lead to be cast onto it, so with the adoption of sliding float techniques float fishing is a method that allows us to cover the coastal waters. Any depth, within certain limits, can be set although float fishing is usually confined to 10 fathoms (18 m) at the most. In addition to the two natural-bait presentation styles, we have spinning. The title means little when compared with spinning in freshwater. In the sea, the use of artificial baits that actually spin is limited. What anglers really do is to *work* the same fishing areas and depths with an artificial lure or bait.

This is an all-action style, where the angler is required to continuously cast and retrieve. He will work his lure over the ground, varying speed of retrieve and depth at which the lure fishes. The baits do not have smell or taste, only action and colour, and it is this combination of manufactured action and angling skill that simulates the actions of a live creature. There are, of course, occasions when the angler will decide to

The layback cast extends the time taken to build up sufficient power in the rod before releasing the weight. The longer time the angler takes to do this gives greater smoothness, so reducing the inefficient, erratic, jerky action that does not give casting distance and can lead to that dreaded overrun and 'bird's nest'.

27

use a natural bait, perhaps a squid or small fish, presented in the spinning—*or working*—fashion. The bait is dead (it may even have been kept for months in a deep freeze) but is made to move through the water in such a way as to deceive alert fish into striking at it as if it were alive. Fly fishing is another possibility, for there are sea species that will accept a concoction of fur and feather, though these fish are relatively few. What I have found is that where fish move in over shallow water, in places like the sandbars found at the mouth of East Coast rivers and where silt deposits have formed a freshwater lagoon, searching fish will take a fly. Bass would be the prime capture but mullet will also move to small flies fished in the surface film.

Rods and reels for shorefishing

All shorecasting rods today are constructed from fibreglass. To be correct, they are of glass-reinforced plastic (GRP). This material can be formed as extruded, tapered solid glass rods or, as is more usual with a casting rod, as hollow glass tubes. To roll a GRP tube, a woven fibreglass cloth is first impregnated with polyester or epoxy resin. The resultant material is then wrapped around a tapered steel mandrel to give it shape and a tapering conformation. The mandrel is then heated in a furnace to allow the resin to permeate throughout the fibres. When cooled, the tube is driven off the mandrel, fitted with spigot (if a joined rod is necessary), rings are whipped on, a handle is fitted and varnished to seal the whippings and give the whole rod a good appearance.

Casting action is dictated by the number of glass wraps, the taper at which they are wrapped and the length of the blank (i.e. hollow) glass tube. Different fishing uses demand a different building principle. Float rods need their power to fight fish only, as there is little weight in the float or bait. Spinning rods are continuously casting so they are stronger in construction. The beachcasting rod is heaviest and strongest, for it is subjected to the greatest stresses and strains. These aren't from the playing and landing of fish—it is the compression during casting which calls for the rod's strength.

Very few fish will put a rod into full compression, though a 6 oz (170 g) lead, properly cast, can bend a rod into a half-circle.

Shorecasting rods

Putting a bait out over the waves can be done with all kinds of beachcasters. To do the fishing well, we anglers attempt to balance our tackle—rod, reel, line and lead—to the prevailing water conditions and the size, or fighting ability, of the fish we expect to catch. Experience has dictated that most shorecasting situations, and their species of fish, fall into three categories:

1. Light Tackle. For fish and current conditions that do not place enormous strains on the rod. Species that do not exceed 12 lb (5 kg), such as bass, codling, flatfish in water where a sinker of 1–3 oz (28–85 g) will suffice.
2. Medium Tackle. The general fishing found all over the British Isles for most shore-caught species up to 30 lb (13 kg). Conditions of tide, seabed and casting distance would need a sinker of 3–5 oz (85–142 g).
3. Heavy Tackle. Used in heavy-water times, when winter gales are piling seas onto the shore or when fishing for the largest of our shore species, tope, winter cod and, possibly, shark. Leads of 5–8 oz (142–227 g) with strong lines are normal.

In addition to the three basic categories of tackle, we have to give some attention to two further factors. The first is concerned with the angler's own attitude to what he is doing: whether he wants simply to catch fish or whether he wishes to catch them in a particular way. Over the past decade a more sporting attitude has grown toward fishing from the shore. Gone are the massive, unbendable poles of the past that gave little satisfaction to the angler when he could hardly feel a hooked fish. So we have lightened our rods and lines accordingly, bringing a heightened awareness of the vibrations and movement given off by the hooked fish, which adds up to a more satisfied angler. Sometimes we find ourselves needing to cast longer distances than usually attained with our chosen rod-line combination. A bass rod, that falls into the light-tackle bracket, will not be able to cast the greater weight demanded to get distance. We have to go up a rod size and strength to get the power to project a heavier lead. Here are some balanced tackles:

Rod	Lead	Reel line	Casting leader breaking strain
10–11 ft (3–3.3 m)	1–3 oz (28–85 g)	12–15 lb (5–7 kg)	18–20 lb (8–9 kg) but not strictly necessary for smooth, gentle casting styles
11–12 ft (3.3–3.6 m)	3–5 oz (85–142 g)	15–18 lb (7–8 kg)	20–30 lb (9–13.5 kg)
11–12 ft (3.3–3.6 m)	5–8 oz (142–227 g)	18–30 lb (8–13.5 kg)	30–60 lb (13.5–27 kg) depending on casting style and fishing possibilities

(Left) *Beach rods can be joined with spigot ferrules, a metal ferrule and counter, or glass-to-glass follow-on joints.*

(Right and far right) *Beach rod rings have to be able to absorb tremendous punishment from the strain of continual casting and yet be light enough so as not to add too much weight to the rod. These typical examples of rings and tip rings are a compromise pattern that ensures function with strength.*

The shorecasting rods in general use today differ little in appearance over the length/casting weight range. Most of them are simple in construction. Two pieces are favoured as the ideal breakdown for transportation, so the rod has to be jointed. Today we use a spigot made from the same fibreglass material as the rod. Metal ferrules are restricted to rods at the cheaper end of the market and for those solid glass rods that are still made.

Rings are important parts of a casting rod. They ease the flow of nylon during casting and spread the pressure load on the rod when a fish is being played into the shore. Rings should be strong but fairly fine in the wire. Too heavy rings can stiffen up a rod where the legs are whipped onto the blank for they will not flex into the curve of a compressed action. And heavy rings add considerable weight to the made-up rod!

Handle styles have changed recently. The fully corked handle is disappearing from a lot of shorecasting rods in favour of plastic or rubber preformed grips. These are fitted at the three positions where the angler's hands go during the cast and retrieve. Those heavy shorecasters that employ an alloy tube, spliced into the glass blanks, do use cork to cover the alloy. There is a choice of two types of reel fitting; the conventional screw winch seat and a flat clip arrangement from the Fuji company. Both do the job perfectly, although neither fitting allows moving the reel position after the rod is made. A lot of shore fishermen simply fix their reels onto the rod using adjustable piping clips.

Float fishing rods

There is little difference between the shore angler's float rod and the coarse fisherman's stepped-up carp or pike rod. In fact, many anglers do

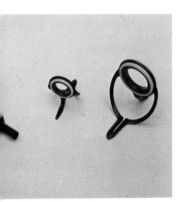

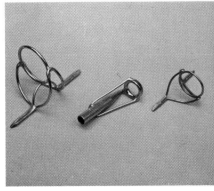

(Right) *Keep all rod rings in perfect condition. A cracked ring will scuff nylon, which can then break at a critical moment.* (Below) *Rod handles vary widely. Modern practice avoids the use of cork, preferring handles of rubber or plastic tubing which is shrunk on to a tight fit.* (Below right) *The traditional screw reel fitting has to fit a particular blank diameter; the Fuji fitting will match any blank.*

Fixing rings to a casting rod

whip toward the ring

insert loop to pull free end under whipping

fix ring into position with clear adhesive tape

glue on tip rings with epoxy resin

(Top left) *The essential part of all fishing—bait. Here, lugworm is being dug from the prolific worm beds in the mud at Clogharne, on Ireland's Dingle Peninsula.* (Left) *The modern shorecaster rod is a slim and light weapon that can be held for hours without any fatigue.* (Above) *Sea fishing float rods must be light enough to be held all day. Such angling calls for quick reactions to a bite and continuous control over the movements of the float and rig in the tide.*

5/0 4/0 3/0 2/0 1/0 1 2 3 4 5 6 7 8 9 10 11 12

use a freshwater rod because there have been few float rods manufactured with the sea angler in mind. Float fishing, whether from a rock platform, harbour wall or trotting down the tide of an estuary, needs a lengthy rod, something that will give good control over what can be a large and powerful fish. Sea fish will fight harder than their freshwater cousins, particularly over the first few fathoms of a run. They also have the added strength of the tide to aid them in their battle for escape. I prefer a rod of 10 ft (3 m) as a minimum length, with a test curve around the 2 lb (1 kg) mark. This will allow me to load the blank with 10–14 lb (4.5–6 kg) nylon, which will handle the toughest fish in the littoral waters. The length of the rod lets me cast reasonably light terminal rigs distances of 40 yd (36 m) or more and controls the final flurries of a hooked fish directly below the rock ledge from which I cast.

When fishing from a harbour wall one has a difficult time landing a fish. Whether a drop net is used or perhaps where a landing net can be taken down steps to the fish, there is always the problem of getting the fish into the net. Very often it has to be held on a tight line. A longish rod has the action necessary to dampen the last desperate lunges that fish make when they see the net. Short rods do not possess this essential characteristic. Trotting a bait needs a rod that has the ability to pick up a lot of line on the strike, and transmit enough power to set the hook. Again the length of rod determines how it can cast and control both tackle and fish. You could use a lighter rod, something like an Avon, but the combined pull of fish and current may be too much for the blank. In slack water times, the length and power of the float rod can be usefully employed as a light casting rod. It will easily throw 1 oz (28 g) bomb and a single lugworm for a bass. As a spinning rod it will have its uses when the rock ledges are high out of the water, for its extra length will give better control of lure and fish close-in.

(Left) A range of brass barrel and link swivels from sizes 5/0 down to 14. This selection will be suitable for any kind of angling situation. (Right) Fishing from a pier or harbour wall demands a dropnet to get the catch to hand. An efficient one can be made by attaching a tube of net to the rim of a bicycle wheel, closing the end with a suitable weight.

Dropnet

The sea spinning rod

Sea spinning lures vary considerably in weight. Many are much larger than the standard freshwater lure. So, a sea angler's spinner needs to have a lot of action. The minimum length is 8 ft (2.5 m) allowing it to cope with fish up to 10 lb (4.5 kg) and to cast baits of $\frac{1}{2}$–1 oz (14–28 g). Rod rings suffer a lot of abuse in both spinning and float fishing so they need to be of adequate proportions. Centred butt and tip rings are not always a good idea. Any fishing from the shore is hard on rings but casting from and scrambling over the ledges puts a lot of stress on the ironmongery. One slip on the rocks and down goes the rod with a crack, something that fragile rings will not absorb. Best are strong, open bridge rings large enough to ensure the smooth passage of stop knots when fishing a float.

The shore angler's reels

There are only two kinds of reel for easy casting. The fixed-spool reel, in a range of sizes, will cover all the fishing styles. It is best when casting light weights as in float fishing and spinning but there can be a case for choosing the fixed-spool when baitcasting. The fixed-spool gives less hassle in use, certainly the 'bird's nest' cannot happen. Many anglers prefer the direct feeling of connection with the fish that the multiplying reel offers. Control of the spool, using a thumb as a sensitive drag, is only possible with this reel. Jamming a finger onto the rim of a fixed-spool can never give the same sense of control, for the line has to drag around the right-angle formed by the bale arm pick-up. The fixed-spool comes into its own at night on the shore. Control of the cast is not as vital with this reel and there is an audible warning of the line slowing down. The noise made as the nylon thrashes out through the rings becomes useful in the hours of darkness. When casting with a multiplier, one has to keep the thumb hovering over the revolving spool to judge just when to arrest the flow of line. Good multiplying reels have bearings that run smoothly and silently, so there isn't much help from the reel in terms of noise.

(Left) *A rod for spinning in the sea needs to be more robust than its freshwater counterpart,* (Right) *Leads required for float-fishing in the sea: drilled bullet and barrel leads to cock a float and an Arlesey bomb for the float-leger techniques, not often possible when sea fishing.*

Filling a reel

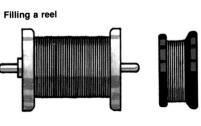

(Above) *There is a weight and size difference between a shore-fishing multiplier and a fixed-spool reel of comparable capacity.* (Above right) *Fill the spool of your reel correctly. There should be sufficient nylon to fill the spool to within 3 mm of the rim on a fixed-spool reel. A multiplier should be loaded to within 6 mm of the gap between spool and side-plates.*
(Right) *Always loosen the drag before float-fishing with a fixed-spool reel, but tighten up when casting a bottom-fishing rig.*
(Bottom right) *The inside parts of a multiplier reel.*

Casting leader knot

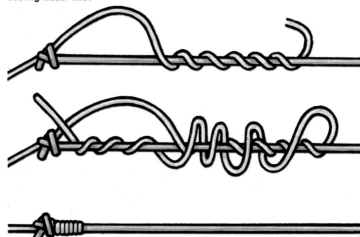

Double-blood knot

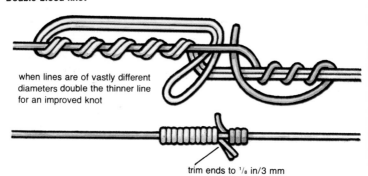

when lines are of vastly different diameters double the thinner line for an improved knot

trim ends to ⅛ in/3 mm

THE SEA ANGLER'S LINES AND KNOTS

In addition to the many knots used by freshwater anglers, the sea fisherman has a number that are particular to his branch of the sport. Sea angling nylon and braided lines are stronger and therefore thicker, so knots have been devised that retain the maximum breaking strain of the line in use. This is especially necessary when braided Dacron or Terylene lines are being joined to swivels or booms as this form of line construction is weakened if the wrong knots are used. The separate fibres, woven to make the braided line, become strangled.

The casting leader knot

In the table on page 29 I have indicated the breaking strains of casting leaders to be joined to the reel line. A leader is vitally necessary to the novice angler and can be equally so to the experienced fisher when casting heavy sinkers or punching out hard to get distance in windy conditions. The leader is a length of heavy gauge nylon knotted onto the reel line to take the increased load put on the line at the time of casting. It also performs the function of giving a strong line to hold a heavy fish on when hauling it through the last short distance of broken water. The leader knot is superb for joining nylon line of unequal diameters such as would be employed when casting a 6 oz (170 g) lead on a line of 18 lb (8 kg) b.s. This knot has the advantage of being slightly tapered, which helps it to pass through the rod rings without catching on the metal. The leader must carry down to the lead. Never put the weight onto thinner nylon as it could crack off with disastrous results on a crowded beach or pier. Only hook droppers should be tied to lesser breaking strain lengths, and here the same line as that on the reel is correct.

To tie a leader knot, take the heavy gauge nylon and form a loop. Pass the end of the reel line through the loop from the back of the circle. Wrap the thin nylon around the leader material five turns. Now, take the free end and thread it through between the first of the twists. Lick both nylon strands and pull the heavy nylon by gripping both the standing line and the loose end. Finish the knot by pulling up on the finer line towards the reel. Cut off the tag ends neatly so that they don't snag the rings or gather minute filaments of weed that can build up to jam in the tip ring. The double-blood knot can be used to join lines but it is not as efficient when the lines are of vastly different thicknesses. A water knot is extremely difficult to use as the length of the leader makes the knot difficult to tie. Leaders vary according to the length of the rod in use, but a yardstick should be that it is the length of the rod from tip ring to reel plus at least 4 ft (120 cm). In conditions of wild wave action, close into the sand or shingle, add another 4–6 ft (1–2 m). This extra length will enable the angler to hold a strong fish against the back surge of waves experienced in these heavy seas.

Most shore fishing situations can be fished with a paternostered bait. This basic rig involves tying in booms, as outriggers, to keep the hook droppers clear of the trace nylon. One could tie in plastic or even wire booms though it is not advisable to over-complicate the rig with needless additions of ironmongery. Hook droppers can be fixed in two ways: on blood loops, or direct to nylon ends that have been tied in with a water knot. Both systems will cope handsomely with species of fish that do not have excessively sharp teeth. To tie the blood loop, take the nylon leader and make a loop in it. Holding the loop in your teeth (I find this a way of providing a third hand), twist the two separate nylon strands over one another for at least four turns. Keep the centre of the windings open to form a wide gap. When the windings are completed, pass the loop (the one that has meantime been trapped in your mouth), through the gap in the windings. Lick the nylon to lubricate the coils and pull up tightly on the lengths of line. The size of the blood loop can be adjusted by the amount of nylon held in the mouth. Hooks can be slipped onto the loop by pushing the nylon through the eye of the hook or by cutting the loop on one side to form a hook dropper. Both of these systems mean that the hook is tied to the leader breaking strain. If you want to drop down in breaking strain, to match the reel line strength, tie the hooks to thinner nylon and slip them over the blood loop.

Hook dropper boom

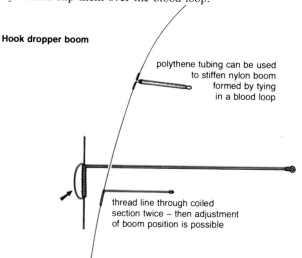

polythene tubing can be used
to stiffen nylon boom
formed by tying
in a blood loop

thread line through coiled
section twice – then adjustment
of boom position is possible

Blood loop

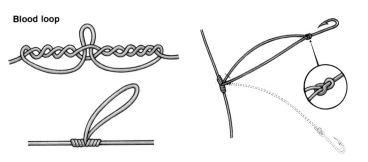

The blood loop is one way in which hook droppers can be fixed on. The text opposite describes how this knot can be tied. The other way of attaching hook droppers is to cut one side of the blood loop and attach the hook by using the tucked half-blood knot, shown on page 40. Both knots are acceptable when seeking those fish species known not to bite through nylon monofilament.

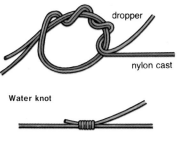

dropper

nylon cast

Water knot

(Left) *Hook droppers can be extended from the trace by a boom of twisted wire or a piece of polythene tubing slipped on to a blood loop to give it stiffness.* (Right) *A simple paternoster made by tying-in two blood loops. Dropper links are added of lesser b.s. nylon joined on with overhand loops.*

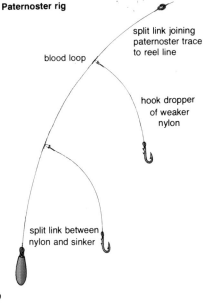

Paternoster rig

split link joining paternoster trace to reel line

blood loop

hook dropper of weaker nylon

split link between nylon and sinker

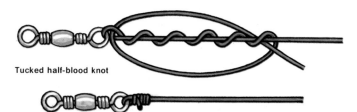

Tucked half-blood knot

The water knot also makes a successful hook dropper, when small lengths of nylon are tied onto the leader material. Begin by holding the weaker nylon length alongside the leader strand. Form a loop in both thicknesses. Then pass both free ends through the loop at least four times. Pull up gradually on both sides of the loop. The hook should be fixed onto the nylon end that is nearest to the rod tip. This end stands out at right angles under the weight of the hook. All swivels, line connectors and hooks are best tied on with the tucked half-blood knot. There are a number of variations to the half-blood knot but I think the one illustrated is probably the best for all sea angling purposes. Hook droppers involve the use of small lengths of nylon, tied to the hook at one end with a tucked half-blood knot and at the other an overhand or figure-of-eight knot gives easy attachment to the paternoster boom.

Knots for braided lines

A lot of sea anglers fill their reels with braided Dacron or Terylene lines. These materials are primarily designed for trolling, when baits are towed behind a boat, or surface fishing such as sharking, where the line is laid on the water surface. Neither line has stretch because it is composed of millions of plaited fibres, so there is no safety margin such as the constant flexing property found when fishing with monofilament. Braided lines require tying with their own knots, designed to prevent sudden breakage from shock loads or when pinched against metal connectors. Braided lines are never connected to hooks, only to swivels or some other form of attachment between reel line and terminal trace. The simplest connection is made by forming a loop at the end of the reel line. This gives the angler a doubled section of reel line, adding strength where most of the wear and rough handling tends to weaken the braid. Most braided lines break without warning when they are subjected to abrasion on the gunwhale or keel of the angling vessel. We guard against this problem by incorporating the doubled leader.

The jammed hangman's knot is ideal for creating a loop which is left as a permanent fixture on the end of the reel line. The best way to tie the knot is by bending a loop around a fixed object that is held in a vice. I use

Jammed hangman's knot

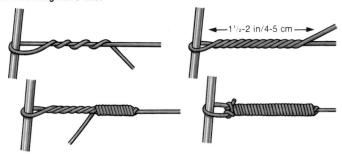

the handle of a screwdriver. The free end of the braided line is twisted over the standing line for at least 2 in (50 mm). Then the free end is bound, tightly, back over the twisted windings. Tie a half-hitch around both of the lines that form the loop. Cut off the loose end leaving $\frac{3}{4}$ in (20 mm). This can be sealed with the end of a lighted cigarette or the flame of a match. The nodule, of hard burned material, will prevent the knot from pulling undone. When really big, strong fish are sought another type of knot becomes necessary. The Policansky knot is, in fact, a method of joining the braided line to a swivelled connector with the minimum of risk from abrasion between line and the metal. Take the doubled end of the line and pass it through the eye of the swivel. I always use a big-game swivel as it has a smoother, larger eye giving a greater diameter for the line to turn around. Bring the doubled line around and over the standing line. Then progressively bind the doubled line over the loop. This ensures that there is a loop of line, protected by the bindings, passing through the eye of the swivel. The reel line is within the bindings so is not subjected to wear as the swivel and line move against one another during the fight. The doubled line could be bound around a nylon thimble when really heavy strains are to be encountered. The American big-game anglers use thimbles and bind the line with leather strips to ward off the abrasion between metal and Dacron.

Policansky knot

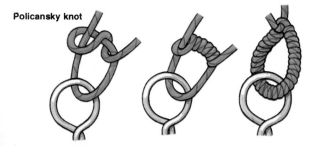

TACKLE FOR BOAT FISHING

Rods

Boat rods are shorter than those used to fish from the shore. There are two reasons for this: boat rods aren't used for casting, and they have to be of a manageable length when fishing from a crowded boat. Boat fishing is conducted in the near-vertical plane—up and down line angles with just slight variations when tide streams a line off from the boat. Power is built into the rod blank for lifting and this strength is concentrated within a 5 ft (1.5 m) working tip section. At least 2 ft (60 cm) is taken up by the handles and winch fitting. Within the limitation of a short working blank, one can see that there must be a number of different types of rod to cope with the variety and size of species met with out on the open sea.

At one time, British rod manufacturers described their rods by titles that inferred what the rod was intended for. 'Tope Fisher', 'Varne' and 'Cod Mark 2' were names that gave a very rough guideline as to the rod's capabilities. Meantime the Americans, through their International Game Fishing Association (IGFA) were establishing line class fishing. They were balancing the use of defined line breaking strains to particular rod blank strengths. The system that has evolved is not perfect but it does give a simple explanation of what a rod can or cannot do in terms of the line. The concept of using the fishing line as the yardstick of measurement is logical because it must be the weakest link between fish and angler. Line breaking strains have been listed as follows:

12 lb (5 kg)	50 lb (22.5 kg)
20 lb (9 kg)	80 lb (36 kg)
30 lb (13.5 kg)	130 lb (59 kg)

It is now a simple choice of balancing the line to the rod IGFA rating. Then, naturally, the angler must decide on the kind of fishing he is going to do and whether the rod/line combination will suit it.

One vital point to remember is that the line breaking strains are not quite as set out above. There is a good reason for this. The IGFA ratings are breaking strains at which the line *must* break, so the line makers build their respective products to break at slightly less than the stated strain— 20 lb (9 kg) b.s. breaks at 18 lb (8 kg), 30 lb (13.5 kg) b.s. breaks at 27 lb (12 kg), and so forth.

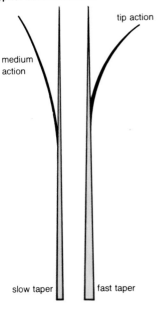

tip action

medium action

slow taper   fast taper

(Left) Boat rod actions: the left-hand rod shows medium action for hard-fighting fish; the right-hand rod has a tip action for a fast strike when bottom fishing. (Below) A rod under heavy strain as a large reluctant common skate is fought at Duny Voe, in the Shetlands.

Rod construction

Boat rods are generally made in two sections with the tip one piece and the butt the other. Very rarely will you find a ferrule or spigot in the middle of the working section, it would be a built-in weakness. The junction is made by fitting the tip into the handle using a locking ferrule that keeps the rod rings perfectly aligned with the winch fitting. Boat rods can be made from both hollow and solid fibreglass. Cheaper rods use the solid, extruded blanks although there is a good case for using a solid glass rod for the dour fighting species such as skate and conger. They place a terrible strain on a hollow glass blank, as both species have a habit of either hugging or tying themselves into the seabed debris. The solid glass blank does not have the recovery, from a harsh curve, that hollow blanks have. They lack positive action.

The well-built hollow glass blank is capable of a wide variety of actions. Alteration in mandrel taper will give tip or all-through action with the possibility of providing local strengthening by judicious cutting of the cloth pattern when the rod is wrapped. I go for a fast taper rod for bottom fishing. Here the tip speed is greater and gives a faster

43

strike action. Tope fishing, or any form of angling where fish make exaggerated fighting movements, needs a little more action along the length of the rod to absorb those desperate lunges, so the medium action rod is used.

Boat rod rings

The kind of rings that a boat rod carries is closely tied to the rod's IGFA rating and the purpose to which it will be put. Light 12 lb (5 kg) class rods need to be fitted with slim, reasonably fine-wired rings that don't add too much weight to the blank. The traditional heavy ring also stiffens a flexing blank somewhat. As the line class of rods increases, so does the strength of the rings. Roller guides appear on the heavier rods where either braided or wire line comes into use. On 50 lb (22.5 kg) class rods we often find roller guides at the tip and butt, with open bridge intermediate rings. The 80 lb (36 kg) and above class rods now carry rollers along their entire length. This is a good ringing system, for the rollers ease the flow of line, cutting down a lot of friction between braid and metal. The acute line angle formed as braided or wire line passes through the normal tulip-type tip ring gives far too much wear on the line. Any sand or mud suspended in the water acts as a grinding compound that will inevitably weaken line. Wire lines, in turn, have a

44

(Left) Four boat rods. Left to right 7ft (2m) Matchmaster Super Nautilus; 8ft (2.5m) Rodcraft Uptide; 6ft (2m) Abu Pacific; 7ft (2m) Achill Sportsman, a rod designed by the author.

(Above right) Heavy rods for skate and shark fishing should be fitted with roller intermediate and top rings. The top ring must be a roller when braided or wire line is used. (Right) Many rods are now fitted with Fuji tip and intermediate rings. This popular range of fittings is claimed to reduce friction on the nylon line and avoid scuffing by virtue of the high-quality, strength and smoothness of the metal.

nasty habit of kinking, sometimes as a result of the sharp angle at the tip ring, but more usually when slack is present between rod tip and sinker.

Rings are made from many materials. Most rods are now fitted with hard-chromed guides. They are strong and hard wearing. Tungsten carbide is an even harder metal but suffers from a certain fragility and will not stand up to hard knocks. The new Fuji rings are eminently suitable for boat rods although they still look a little too unconventional for some rods. Aftco roller guides are made from stainless steel with hardened rollers. Very little service is required to the moving parts but the guides benefit from regular cleaning and lubrication.

Lightweight, hard-chrome rings are suitable for 12lb (5kg) and 20lb (9kg) class rods. There must be enough rings to spread the load along the working length of the rod. At the maximum curve of the rod the line must not touch the body of the rod.

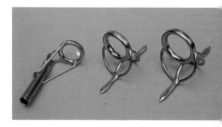

(Above) *A boat rod doing its job with the power in the blank being tested against the muscle of the fish.* (Left) *The length of the rod handle must allow the angler to rest the side plate of the reel against his left forearm for stability and prevent 'rock and roll' while retrieving line.* (Below) *A boat centrepin, the Alvey 525 C52. This model is fitted with a slipping clutch and possesses a tremendous rate of line retrieve. The spool is made from fibreglass.*

Handles used always to be fully corked. Now we see many rods that have composite grips giving a good 'feel' to the rod. There are a number of reel fixing methods in use. The position of the reel fitting is of the greatest importance as it affects the whole of one's fishing. The centre of the reel and position of the handle are critical to the way in which you control the various functions of the reel while playing a fish or when recovering line. I find that a butt length of around 16 in (40 cm) is right. With the reel at that distance from the butt cap my left hand is just about fully extended with the right hand comfortably closed over the handle of the reel. The side of a multiplying reel lies against my left forearm, preventing the rocking motion that winding can induce.

Reels for boat fishing

If we discount the fixed-spool reel as only having a place as an occasional spinning instrument, we find that there are only two styles of reel; the centrepin and the multiplier. Providing that the particular reel is of good quality with fine spindles, well-machined gears and a clutch that works, either of the reels will do a perfect job at sea. The centrepin gives a good line recovery rate, due to its large diameter and has, in recent times, become rather sophisticated. Centrepins can now be bought with star drag, giving adequate clutch control with a slipping facility. Older centrepins had a direct drive. This meant that a fish pulling line rapidly from the reel could jerk the handle out of the angler's hand. The handle spun wildly and if any attempt was made to grab it one often had badly rapped knuckles. Probably the most favourable point about centrepin reels is that they do not have machined gears to worry about. The spindle is simply driven through the drum and located within sensible bearings.

On the other hand, multiplying reels are complicated. They have a gear train, by which the turning of the handle transmits a multiplied number of winds to the spool; they are geared up, which places a great strain on the master gear and pinion. All multipliers used at sea have a free spool facility, to enable the terminal gear to be lowered to the seabed, and a slipping clutch. The clutch operates by sandwiching a number of soft washers between metal plates that alternately drive or slip. The soft washers are compressed by the star drag wheel so that they convey the motion of the handle through to the gears. Should the weight of a fish or the power of its fight overcome the drag setting, the washers will slip to release the strain on the gears. That is what is intended by the reel designers, but anglers tend to abuse this kind of reel. They apply massive force onto the handle, using it like a winch instead of pumping the rod to regain line. Setting the drag on a multiplying reel is a simple task. Presupposing a line breaking strain of 30 lb (13.5 kg), the clutch ought to slip at 20 lb (9 kg) as a maximum setting. Thread the line through the rings and get a companion to pull line off against a spring balance until the correct setting is achieved. Star drags are difficult to return to the same setting if it has been altered but reels with a lever drag are better as the angler can return the drag setting accurately using the visual indicators on this type of multiplier.

Most of the problems that occur with reels used by sea anglers are due to abuse, and corrosion caused by saltwater. These reels must be regularly serviced, and washing in freshwater after every trip is essential, with periodic lubrication of all the moving parts.

Hooks, lines and sinkers

The sea angler has his own patterns and sizes of hooks. There are hundreds of types in use by European anglers. When you consider the numbers of different fish that we catch, the hooks must vary tremendously. Shark upwards of 100 lb (45 kg) down to mullet are all catered for by the hook makers. Hooks are made of steel, some of fairly soft bent wire and others of forged wire. These two materials have different characteristics; the bent wire will straighten out with a heavy load, whereas the forged wire might snap. The choice is one of use, size of fish

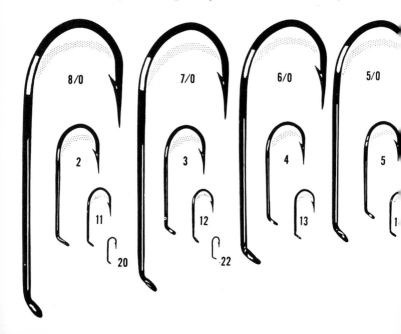

(Above) *Multiplying reels for boat fishing. Left to right: Winfield Nautilus 30; Penn 4/0; Abu 9000C; Mitchell 622. (Above right) Oil your reels through the nipples, but do not overdo it or the clutch will tend to slip under pressure. (Right) The lever drag's advantages lie in the angler being able to set the drag to predetermined strike and fish-fighting tensions.*

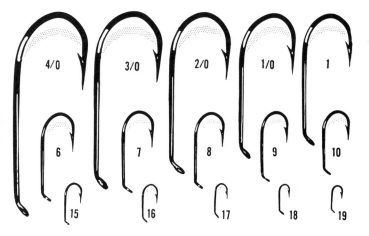

This is the range of the famous Mustad-Viking hooks all shown in full size. There are Mustad hooks for every kind of fishing style.

and what you can afford. I prefer expensive forged, fine wire hooks and I only use them once. A short, needle-sharp point with a shallow-cut barb and reasonable length of shank will suit most sea angling purposes. Avoid heavy wire hooks—they need too much striking force to get them to penetrate. A 'rank' barb, one that juts out from the body of the hook, will account for a lot of lost fish. You strike, feel the weight of the fish and then it is gone. What has happened is that the point went in up to the swelling of the barb but with the fish's movement, as it felt the hook, it twisted out again.

Anybody could be forgiven for becoming mesmerised by the fantastic array of fishing hooks offered today. Sooner or later a choice has to be made by the individual angler. I made mine some years ago, so I illustrate them here. I do not suggest that they are best for all anglers, but the patterns have been good to me! I have settled on only four patterns for all of my sea angling activities. The first, the Mustad 7780c, copes with most boat fishing apart from the very large and powerful species. This pattern is made from 6/o size down to 20, which means that I can use them for conger, tope and general fishing in the middle sizes. Wrasse call for a size 2–4 in the same pattern. This hook is made from forged wire, has a bronzed finish, and reversed superior hook point, with a tapered, turned down eye. All of that is needed to describe the kind of hook that it is!

I use fine-wire Aberdeen hooks for bass fishing and other shore angling applications where a springy iron is thought necessary. The Aberdeen is perfectly shrouded within a single rag or lugworm. A long-shanked Kirby hook comes in handy when fishing for flats, their small mouths create a problem of hook removal. This pattern is also used to dress mackerel feathers, which are chicken feather held onto the shank with bindings of monofilament nylon. My last pattern is for big fish, species that put enormous strains on tackle and men. The Mustad Seamaster hook is known around the world, and found in every

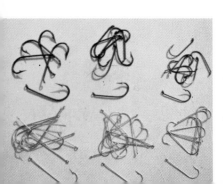

(Left) *The author's choice of hook patterns, from the Mustad range. Top row: Viking hooks. A forged, reversed pattern for general boat and shore fishing; bottom row: Aberdeen pattern hooks. These are fine wire, fairly long-shanked models for shore fishing.*

angler's box that goes aboard a deepsea or big-game boat. It is incredibly strong and durable, and is made in a wide range of sizes, though 10/0–2/0 are the sizes most often used for shark, skate, conger and game species.

There are four distinct kinds of fishing line used in sea angling. Nylon is by far the most popular, as it is cheap and strong for the fine diameter. The amount of stretch varies from one maker to another but it can be a safety margin for the beginner to the sport. It is important to remember that nylon with a low stretch factor has a poor knot strength unless the knots are of the correct type and well tied. Stretchy line has a better knot strength and can be said to be more tolerant of the badly tied knot! I do not find that colour of line is at all important to the success of my fishing. Braided lines are larger in diameter when compared with nylon lines of similar breaking strain. Added to this, they have millions of interference surfaces, where the woven fibres provide little pockets of resistance to the passage of the tide. This means that a braided line needs more lead to hold bottom. There is little or no stretch, which gives little room for error on the part of the angler. But the power of the strike is more positive than could be imparted on a nylon monofilament line.

When the tide is so strong as to demand extremely heavy weights, or it carries the terminal rigs way back downtide where bite detection

(Right) *This is the big-game angler's choice of hook. It is the Mustad Seamaster, and is hand-forged steel to cope with the massive power of big sharks, specimen conger and common skate.* (Below) *These are long-shanked flatfish hooks, some already tied to nylon droppers.*

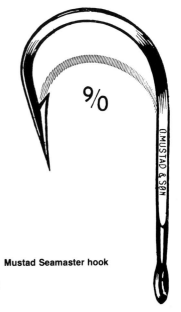

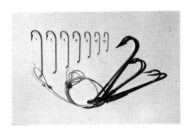

Mustad Seamaster hook

51

becomes impossible, a wire line might be the answer. It is fine in thickness and has its own weight throughout the length needed to reach bottom. Striking is absolutely positive because there is no stretch at all and the bites are almost 'telegraphed' up to the angler. But a wire line suffers from two pitfalls: it kinks if not kept taut at all times, and it needs a length of nylon between the wire and the terminal rig to ensure that you don't strike out of the fish. Great care must be taken in handling the line. Under strain, such as when the sinker gets fixed into the seabed debris, *never* attempt to pull the lead out by grasping the wire. It can cut through a hand like a wire through cheese.

The last type of fishing line is an amalgam between braided line and soft lead wire. The lead provides a core through the centre of the woven material where it gives weight in use. The Americans use this lead-cored line when trolling to take the bait down below the water's surface. It doesn't really have a place in our bottom fishing, so it is disappearing gradually from the market. The illustration (below) gives a theoretical idea of the curves between rod tip and terminal rig when using the four lines, always assuming that the same weight of sinker is involved. To sum up, I would say that nylon is the best all-round line for bottom fishing. Braided Dacron or Terylene is useful for sharking or any fishing where the fish runs hard in mid-water away from rough ground *and*

Fishing in a strong tide creates a belly in the line from rod tip to seabed. Here we see three theoretical curves from lines: Wire line (A) cuts tide easily, whereas nylon (B) and braided line (C) take a longer path in the pull of the tide.

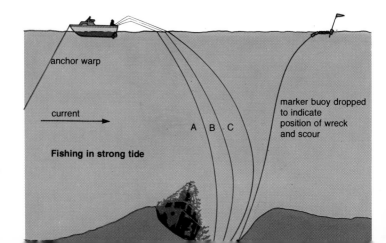

anchor warp

current

A B C

Fishing in strong tide

marker buoy dropped
to indicate
position of wreck
and scour

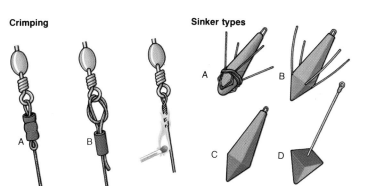

Crimping

Sinker types

(Above left) *Flexible wire can be fixed to a swivel by two systems, A or B. Fine nylon-covered trace wire can be welded by heating the covering until it melts.* (Above right) *Sinkers: (A) bomb; (B) square torpedo; (C) shore-casting lead; (D) Sandfast.*

where perfect contact with the fish is called for. Wire line will combat strong tidal currents but special rod rings are necessary to stand up to the constant wear.

We need weights to get the bait down to the fish or out over the waves when shorecasting. Size is important but so is shape. A lead does two things: it takes the bait to where the fish are *and* it should keep it there. You will see round, watch-type grip leads that have little pimples around them. These are intended to get a grip in soft sand and mud. The conical lead has its centre of gravity in the bottom of the lead. It gets down fast but tends to roll around when the current is strong. The shorefisherman's torpedo lead is good for boat fishing as well. Though intended to fly through the air easily, by reason of its aerodynamic shape, the streamlined shape offers little resistance to strong tide when used as a boat lead. It also pulls out of rock a lot easier than the portly, conventional boat sinkers.

When boat fishing in a strong tide, one often uses so much lead that the weight smothers all bite vibrations, and can overload the rod blank. Sometimes two sinkers, instead of a single lead, avoid these problems. Seamen know that two small anchors will often hold the ground better than one big one. Even a shorefisherman's wired grip lead can be used, providing the rig keeps the sinker away from the terminal tackle on the drop down.

Shore fishing needs one type of lead only when bait is being cast. The

53

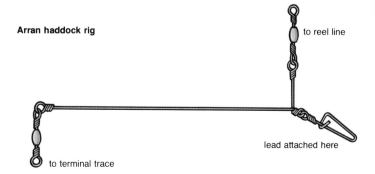

Arran haddock rig

to reel line

lead attached here

to terminal trace

streamlined torpedo lead has its centre of gravity in the right place, near to the leading tip of the lead. It will not tumble through the air and holds in all but the strongest currents. When the tide does get too much for the torpedo lead, change to a grip version of the same pattern and size. But don't chop and change between sizes of sinker, it will alter the casting characteristics of your rod and change the flowing movement of your cast. Most rods are best used with one size of sinker, then casting becomes automatic. A grip lead can put a lot of stress onto the rod when the sinker is being wound in. The 'Breakaway' pattern has altered all that. Before winding in, a sharp tug releases the beads from their locating holes thus turning the grip wires back on themselves where they give no resistance to the seabed. You can make a breakout lead with swivelling wires that have to be bent after insertion into a drilled hole. The wires are set by a rubber band that slips off under a sharp tug.

Float fishing needs drilled leads that can be attached to the reel line below the float. Drilled bullets or barrel weights will do the job, especially when a sliding float technique is called for. In shallow water, with a fixed float, the freshwater SSG split shot will suffice. Casting spinning lures sometimes needs the addition of a lead on the terminal trace. I prefer to use a spiral or Wye lead, and especially the latter as it doesn't work its way free from the line.

Bits and pieces

The average sea angler's tackle box is filled with little bits of metal and plastic—some of them necessary! Most of this collection of gadgets will be concerned with making the sinker slide freely, booming the hooks away from the reel line or connecting various lines and tackle items together.

Booms

They can be separated into those that slide and those that are fixed onto the line to support other tackle. The Clement's boom is intended to

54

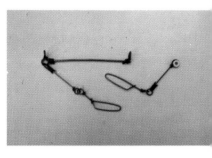

(Left) *The Arran haddock rig is a fixed leger boom that relies on a fish pulling the bait against the sinker.* (Right) *The booms most used in sea fishing: the double-eyed Clement's boom and the Kilmore, which is more prone to tangle in a slackish current. They are both available with or without porcelain eyes.*

carry a sinker and slide on the running line. Some are made in plain metal, usually blackened brass wire, while the better quality booms have porcelain eyes inserted in the two ringed eyes. But the eyes often crack under stress or when rattled around in the tackle box, and if this isn't detected they can easily cut the reel line! There is little advantage in this type of boom over the plain metal Clement's as the free-running property is doubtful. Anyway, they are all lubricated when immersed in water! Always take care when attaching the Clement's boom to keep the lead from fouling the terminal rig.

A Kilmore boom is just a simplified, single-eyed version of the Clement's boom. Again we find the porcelain insert with, possibly, the same trouble. The Kilmore cannot keep the lead away from the rig quite so easily when the bait is being lowered. A heavy gauge link swivel will do a similar job and it's a lot cheaper! There are a multitude of other bits and pieces involved in sea angling. Where they are important they will be mentioned in a fishing context in the following sections of this book.

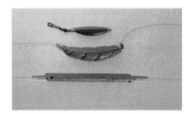

(Right) *Spinning and trolling weights: top, the Wye; centre, the spiral; below, the Newark.* (Below right) *A major advance in shore fishing was the lead called the Breakaway. The grip wires are held in place by small beads that sit in tiny hollows in the body. A sharp tug on the rod pulls the wires free from the body to allow them to fold back. Free from the mud or sand they come up easily.*

Bass

(Above) *Gameness and food value are the attributes of the bass.*
(Below) *Bass fishing in rolling surf on an Irish storm beach.*

SALTWATER FISH SPECIES

Bass *Dicentrarchus labrax*

This fish is one of the most highly prized and praised of British shore species. Of course, bass are caught offshore though fishing for them is usually confined to working reefs with artificial baits or inshore dinghy angling. Powerful, muscular, hard-scaled and large finned, the bass works the shoreline in strong water for its food. The bass is easily identified. The predominant colour is a clean silver on the flanks, blending into a creamy-white belly. On the back, especially on mature fish, the scales are a rich purple-black. There are two distinct dorsal fins of equal length. The first is spiked, giving the clue that this sea fish belongs to the perch family. The rearward dorsal is soft-rayed. There is a black blotch on the gillcase which has a vicious cutting edge. Bass are found off the south and west of the British Isles. Very rarely will a bass be caught north of Yorkshire or the Mull of Galloway. It seems that when small the species prefers clean, saline water, while ageing fish enter the brackish water that is present in estuaries.

Bass move into shallow water as it warms in the sunshine of late spring. Water hardly covering the backs of the fish will be scoured for worms, small fish and shellfish. Generally, there will be more bass on a rocky coast as it offers a more productive feeding area but when the ocean movement creates a swell that breaks onto the storm beaches, the bass will move onto the clean ground seeking creatures that are pounded out from the sand. It is on these beaches that the majority of bass anglers go for their sport. There is something spellbinding about the regular turning of the breakers. Standing thigh-deep in the surf adds another dimension to shore fishing! Bass fishing from the shallow-gradient storm beaches demands light tackle. Whether wire-gripped or other-wise, a 4 oz (113 g) weight will take bait out and hold the ground. To get the best out of the fight and give the angler the kind of mobility necessary on the strand, an 11 ft (3.3 m) rod that is light in the hand is best. Even a stepped-up carp rod has a place in this kind of fishing. It is perfectly capable of casting 2 oz (56 g) which will hold in times of slack water on the surf beach. Choice of reels is one of personal preference. I like the multiplier for most beachcasting applications although, with light leads of about 1 oz (28 g), the fixed-spool becomes a better casting instrument. The fixed-spool handles small sinkers more easily.

Over open, clean ground, bass fishing offers a simple choice of terminal rig; either a nylon paternoster or running leger. There isn't a great difference between the two rigs in use. On balance, I think the

paternoster will be less likely to tangle, both in the cast and when a lateral current washes the bait along the beach. At all costs avoid the leger system that runs the sinker on the reel line! The hook trace often wraps around the main line during the cast, which defeats the purpose of a running leger rig. It is better to have the lead suspended on a short nylon link. This construction allows the use of a wired sinker within the running leger principle. Two hooks are enough on the paternoster rig, with one on a running leger. To use more hooks and bait will mean that you increase the amount of drag as the terminal gear is cast. Inevitably, to overcome the drag one would have to go up a size with the sinker and that would defeat the whole purpose of a light tackle attitude.

Bass fishing on an open strand is a mobile business. The fish feed their way, progressively, along the breakers. Anglers can keep in touch with the moving fish by walking along the strand, making a cast, fishing it out, then recasting. The system is easier to work if there are a number of anglers fishing together. As one gets a bite, followed by another bait taken, the pattern of fish feeding and direction of travel will emerge. All the anglers have to do is to leapfrog beyond one another, keeping in touch with the fish. Many bass fishers will tell you to cast beyond the third breaker. This may well be where fish are but not always. Obviously the breaking surflines do provide the pounding effect on the sandy bottom that forces the worms and sandeels out of the sand but bass will come in much closer to the beach. It is not unusual to find fish swimming in the flat tables of water that are running in from the last breaker to turn over. I've had bass swimming behind me when I have been casting from thigh-high water.

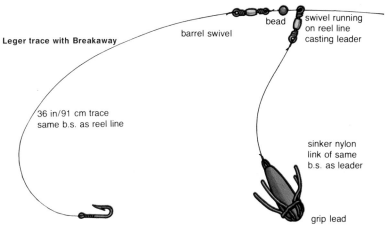

Leger trace with Breakaway

barrel swivel

bead

swivel running
on reel line

casting leader

36 in/91 cm trace
same b.s. as reel line

sinker nylon
link of same
b.s. as leader

grip lead

(Above left) *In bass fishing the rod must be held at all times, for
bites are lightning fast.* (Above) *Strong currents call for a leger
trace with Breakaway sinker and swivels to help avoid line twist
when the rig rolls across the seabed.* (Below) *When there is little
surf on the open strand, the author prefers to fish from rocky points
into deeper water. Bass will often change their feeding habits,
leaving the worms of the sands for the crabs and small fish that live
on or near the weed-covered rocks.*

No surf—no bass, is often the case on a storm beach. Certainly that statement can be true during the hours of daylight. But at night, bass will venture into shallow water when there is not so much as a trickle of surf. Bass have a varied diet which means that the species cover a variety of feeding habitats. At each end of a west-facing beach there is often a rocky point. The coast of Britain and Ireland is broken up by sandy beaches that nestle between cliffs. As they leave the strands to patrol along the edges and rough ground that form the base of the cliff buttresses the fish can be taken by other methods. Here, float fishing and spinning techniques apply. The angler must change to baits that feeding bass are likely to encounter. Crabs, soft and in the peeling stage, are on the fish's menu along with shellfish and crustaceans.

The float fisher can introduce shrimps and prawns as a hook bait. Strips of mackerel floatfished down the tide will often become interesting to fish that would ignore the same bait if it were fished a good distance away in the open surf. All fish expect to find particular food in certain places, so we must give them what they are looking for. Where there are shoals of fry, spinning can be a productive technique. This applies more for school bass than for the larger specimens which don't often chase a spinning lure. But what they *will* move to is a spun natural bait that is fished sink-and-draw. Sprats, fixed to a spinning flight, are a beautiful lure for the big predatory fish.

(Right) *Freshly caught bass being de-scaled before being prepared for the oven. This fish is highly prized for its excellent eating qualities.* (Below) *Sprats make a good sink-and-draw bait and stay on the hook through a good number of casts.*

Sprat sink-and-draw bait

trace ends in a nylon loop taken through the hook eye and around the body of the bait

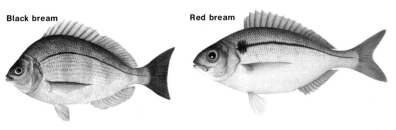

Black bream

Red bream

Sea bream

Two species of sea bream are to be found in the waters of the North-East Atlantic. These are the black bream *Spondyliosoma cantharus* and red bream *Pagellus bogaraveo*. Both fish are annual visitors, arriving with the warmer water of late spring as travellers on the North Atlantic drift. The black bream is a deep-bodied, flattened fish with a pronounced hump to the upper body. The male fish exhibits sparkling blue flanks interspersed with vertical bars of dark scales. The clarity of colour soon disappears after death, when the male fish resembles the drab black-grey of the female. Scientists say that black bream have an hermaphrodite stage in their lives, the suggestion being that the fish is male *and* female during its life. The lateral line is a broad, sharply curved line without any other dark markings. Nearly half of the rays forming the dorsal fin are spined, with the sharp spikes leading soft rays towards the tail. There are also three spines forming the leading rays of the anal fin.

Apart from the rich red coloration of the red bream, its large eyes and a black spot at the beginning of the almost straight lateral line make the species easy to identify. It is a sleeker fish with a bigger mouth than the black bream. Both species are to be found off the south and west coasts of the British Isles from May onward. We know that the black bream gathers off the coast to breed in selected areas but the red bream has a wider distribution, making accurate spawning grounds hard to pinpoint. It is said that the red bream spawns in winter. Our two sea breams are a small representation of an enormous family of over 200 species but most of them confined to warmer, equatorial waters.

Sea bream haunt rocky ground, especially when there is a depth of water from the seabed. Over pinnacles or a wreck, these plucky fighters swim around the tips of the underwater obstructions. They are shoaling species, tending to mass up at clearly defined heights above other reef-dwelling fish. Because of this one has to discover the depth at which bream are swimming. After hooking a fish, the tackle must be lowered to exactly that distance to regain the shoal. There are a number of ways in

which this can be achieved. Some reel makers incorporate a device which measures off the run. There is at least one make of nylon line having different colours for each 33 ft (10 m), or so, of line on the spool. I prefer to use a simpler, better system. I tie on a nylon stop knot in fine monofilament when I've found my fish. Then it's a simple matter of running line off until the stop knot catches my thumb. The knot can be slipped up or down the line according to the depth at which bites are felt. With attention, the method can be effective in ensuring that a similar depth is searched on each cast.

Bream can be caught on standard paternostered baits providing the bait and hook are small enough for these fish (that do not have very large mouths), to take the offering easily. Any bait that is too large will be gradually whittled down, with false bites that cannot be struck. I like using a long flowing trace carried down by a spiral or similar weight. One hook is sufficient with a fine slip of mackerel bait.

In practice the line need not be more than about 6 lb (3 kg) b.s.

Stop knot

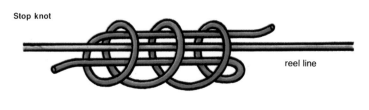

reel line

leave 1/8 in/3 mm tags

(Far left) Black bream caught during the species' migration to the South Coast of England. (Left) A red bream of 6 lb (3 kg) caught off Achill Island, Co Mayo, Ireland. (Right) A large ragworm makes fine bream bait, and is best when presented on a two-hook Pennell tackle. (Below left) The stop knot allows a careful correction of float-fishing depth as it slides freely.

Ragworm bait

However, I use 10 lb (4.5 kg) balanced to an 8 ft (2.5 m) sea spinning rod and multiplier. That extra line strength gives the opportunity to search over the tip of a pinnacle where I just might get into a pollack, or some other larger specimen than I bargained for! I think that pollack push the fry up to where the bream are waiting so the angler has the chance of further species. Thread the fish slip high onto the shank of the hook. Bream are notorious for eating their way up a long lash, leaving the angler with a minute piece on the hook bend that the fish doesn't want or is suspicious of. One can either use a baitholder hook, where the snecked shank will take a purchase on the bait, or pull the bait up over the eye and knot. It's probably a sound idea to leave a short stub of nylon at the knot to act as a stop to the bait. Sea bream rate very highly as sporting species. Both bream will give a head-jagging response to light tackle, boring deep with thrilling runs that can test you. They also taste magnificent when cooked on the bone, and served with a piquant shrimp sauce. Don't take more bream than you need.

Coalfish *Pollachius virens*
A handsome fish of great fighting quality that inhabits deep water in more northerly climes than its close relative the pollack. There is some confusion between the two species. Though similar in shape and

habitat, the coalfish is a dark, steely black on the upper body graduating to a creamy-white underbelly. Its lateral line is absolutely straight and white in colour. The jaws are of equal length. Coalies—and this is only one of the many names given to the fish on a regional basis—grows to larger sizes than the pollack. The British rod-caught fish record is constantly rising, as a result of increased angling activity over the big fish wrecks. On our side of the Atlantic Ocean the record stands at just over 33 lb (15 kg) but across the Atlantic the rod-caught record for the species is $46\frac{1}{2}$ lb (21 kg). Commercial fishermen have told me neither of these rod-caught records comes anywhere near what they have seen in a professional's catch. Coalfish are more widely distributed than the pollack. They spread from the Bay of Biscay to Iceland and the far North of Norway. West Atlantic populations inhabit the coast of North America and the southern tip of Greenland.

Although large coalfish are associated with rocky ground, the adult fish make migratory journeys to follow herring and sprat shoals. Coalies are principally fish feeders whereas the pollack takes crustaceans and shellfish from the reefs and worms over open ground. The coalfish is a species that the angler has to seek. Habitat and its identification is vitally important when fishing for coalfish. I have found that they swim slightly deeper than pollack. On a reef, pollack feed over the tip of the pinnacles. Coalies seem to spend their time at the rock faces that form the body of the reef. A similar pattern appears when wreck fishing. Of course, larger specimens of both species live and feed lower down in the water. This is because they both predate on small fish that use the same reef as a habitat. Ambush is generally from the darker, deeper water up toward the light. This behavioural trait can be emulated when fishing for the coalfish. Using a two-hook paternoster, with natural bait or two artificial eels, the rig can search the top and down the face of the reef. Because of the foul ground and the chance of snagging the lead, it is wise to attach the lead weight using a 'Rotten Bottom'. This is a nylon link of lesser breaking strain. It is a means of saving expensive terminal tackle. If the rig gets stuck on the bottom, only the sinker will be lost as the weaker nylon breaks. I have found that a 20 lb (9 kg) class outfit will cope with all but the most strenuous angling. If your chosen fishing has also produced ling of any size, a change to 30 lb (13.5 kg) gear would combat their strength and size. Like most members of the cod family, coalfish fight hardest over the first few fathoms of line recovery and it is at this time that tackle is given its hardest test. A fish that is hooked on or near to a reef knows where security lies and it will endeavour strongly to get back to the reef. The fish must be held on its first powerful rush, then lifted to

(Right) *Two specimens taken on the same paternoster trace, a coalfish and a pollack. The boat is drift-fishing over the prolific grounds of a great Irish angling mark, Achill Island, Co Mayo.*
(Below) *Artificial sandeels are lifelike and efficient lures over reefs and wrecks. Distance between the booms on the reel line should be sufficient to avoid hooks or lures snagging the other.*

'Rotten bottom' weak link

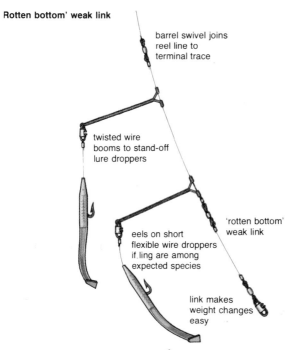

barrel swivel joins reel line to terminal trace

twisted wire booms to stand-off lure droppers

eels on short flexible wire droppers if.ling are among expected species

'rotten bottom' weak link

link makes weight changes easy

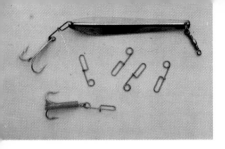

Newark Positive Poundage links join hooks to lures with a guaranteed breakout strain to save the body of the lure.

To avoid losing treble hooks attach them with a nylon link of lower b.s. than the reel line as a breakout link.

turn it away from the flight direction. But don't tighten the clutch too hard! The natural arc of the rod may not give enough spring to allow for those first wild rushes so it is far better to adjust the slipping drag to take account of any movements that may break the line. A thumb, hovering over the spool, is a much finer adjuster of line slipping tension and should be used to counteract the thrashing of a strong fighting fish.

Coalfish will take pirks as they give that metallic flash and vibration that simulates the actions of a live fish. Fishing over reef or wreck will inevitably bring the treble hook of a pirk into contact with weed and rock crevices. That means a lost pirk! The problem can be averted by introducing a nylon breakout link of lower breaking strain than the reel line between the pirk and hook, or a metal link can be inserted. There is a new link, called the Positive Poundage Link, that is in guaranteed breaking strains. It's ideal for the angler who regularly fishes on the productive but foul ground of a rocky bottom or underwater hulk.

Cod *Gadus morhua*

Of all the marine species the cod must receive more angling effort throughout the year than any other fish. It is also the principal commercial fish, attracting the attention of most of the North Atlantic trawlermen. Despite man's predation on the species, cod remain the most constant of fish. Each season the deepwater specimens migrate to the British inshore waters where many of them spawn in water of 30 fathoms (55 m) or more. During the winter these same fish are likely to be found in depths of only a few fathoms as they follow sprat and herring shoals. Although essentially a bottom feeder, the cod will rise in the water to harry shoals of pelagic fodder fish.

Cod are not the prettiest of our marine fish. Thick in the fore part, the

Cod

fish has a huge head which seems out of proportion to its rear end, particularly when the fish has spawned. The body slims down markedly from a point behind the vent. This species varies tremendously in coloration. Large Atlantic cod are yellow with brownish blotches divided by a broad, white lateral line that curves gently over the pectoral fins. Not all cod are migratory, those that live close to our rocky shores adopt a colouring similar to that of their habitat. A rich, reddish brown cod will be found in areas of thick kelp. It is thought that these juvenile residents migrate after a few years of inshore feeding. Then they change body colour to match that of the well-known oceanic kind.

March into April are the popular months for cod spawning. The females release huge numbers of eggs, several millions being deposited from a fish weighing 10 lb (4.5 kg) or more. The species matures at 3–4 years, when they measure just over 24 in (60 cm). Cod have an omnivorous diet, they'll eat practically anything although a close inspection of stomach content will indicate a preference for crabs and other crustaceans. Inshore, a cod will search for marine worms and shellfish. The species changes its diet depending on the availability of other foods. Sprats, herring and small mackerel will be sought when shoals of these species move across a cod holding ground. Look to the mud or sandy bottom for the cod, especially where are clumps of weed or outcrops of broken ground that can produce the sort of food the cod likes. In deeper water, large specimens will haunt wrecks and reefs where the fish population provides a continuous and easily caught feast. Off the shore, cod feed near beaches where a strong tide scours worms from the littoral zone. Around rocky coasts the fish feed on the many forms of invertebrate life that find sanctuary in weedbeds or among the numberless crevices in the foul ground.

Fishing from the shore

Cod are not known for their fighting ability. What they are adept at doing is feeding in areas of strong tidal current. Anglers' recognition of this behaviour has led to a specialized cod fishing tackle set-up. Hollow fibreglass rods of 12 ft (3.5 m), capable of casting a 6 oz (170 g) weight

67

with a multiplying or fixed-spool reel loaded with 18 lb b.s. (8 kg) nylon. A casting leader is always employed to offset the shock load applied to the tackle by vigorous casting techniques. Keeping the bait on the seabed, where cod can find it in the tidal pressure, often means using weights with grip wires that dig into the sand to prevent the terminal rig from being swept in an arc down the tide. The end tackle can be either of paternoster or leger conformation. Either system will present the bait where the fish are feeding—hard on the bottom. In strong water there is little to choose between the different rigs, though fishing a slack water gives an edge to the legered bait, for it allows a fish to pick up the bait and then move off before feeling a resistance from the line. I use two hooks on a paternoster rig (see page 39) and a single hook on a link leger.

Cod have big mouths capable of swallowing large baits. Even the

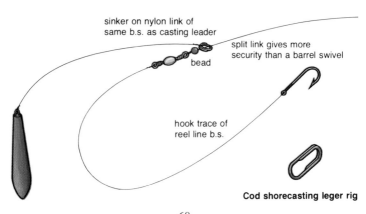

sinker on nylon link of
same b.s. as casting leader

split link gives more
security than a barrel swivel

bead

hook trace of
reel line b.s.

Cod shorecasting leger rig

68

inshore codling is well able to take a multi-worm bait threaded onto a 6/o hook. I've adopted this size of hook for all my cod fishing. There are times when lighter tackle systems are called for, when fishing in situations where there is little if any tide or natural hazard to overcome. Then I drop my tackle down in strength to 12 lb (5 kg) line on a 4 oz (113 g) casting bass rod. The gear gets lighter but the hook size remains the same. What *does* change is the hook pattern. From a forged Viking, I move to an Aberdeen hook that is extremely fine in the wire. The worms are then threaded up the snood, above the hook, rather than offered as a bunch. Long casting is associated with fishing for cod. Heavy winter weather and the number of anglers now fishing from the shoreline determine where the fish will be feeding. A heavy surge onto the shore will keep fish at distance, where they can collect the worms and other food driven out of the ground by the pounding action of the waves. Also, a lot of anglers hurling rigs out create a considerable disturbance. Noise, created as the leads hit the water, is often the key to where feeding fish will be. They will move out from the shoreline, avoiding the noise so the man who can cast long distances has a better chance of getting his bait among fish. However, I'm not suggesting that long casting is always necessary when cod fishing, for there will be many situations where this species will be found feeding almost on the beach.

Lugworm must be the best of the cod baits. It has those vital ingredients to pull fish: smell and a natural appearance combined with reasonable availability to the angler. There are many other hookbaits that will attract cod. As I said earlier, this species will take practically

(Above left) *The author with a first-class cod from a wreck off Stonehaven, North East Scotland.* (Left) *A shore-casting leger rig for cod, with a split link used to provide a sliding leger facility when vigorous casting may break a barrel swivel.* (Right) *The sea angler's standard winter cod offering, lugworms. Sometimes 'cocktails' of lug and squid, or lug and fish strip, are found to work when single baits fail to attract feeding fish.*

(Left) *Leslie Moncrieff, who pioneered the Layback method of shorecasting, with a catch of prime cod from Kent's well-known Dungeness beach.*
(Right) *Casting leader knots are vital additions to a rig when it is necessary to cast sizeable leads to a distance.*

anything that they find. When sprat shoals come inshore the cod will feed exclusively on these tiny fish. Then we have to adapt our casting rig to cater for the fact that sprats are soft so are easily cast off the hook. A simple loop attachment will hold the sprat to the hook, trapping the tail wrist to prevent the bait flying off as the sinker drags it through the air. Cod fishing can be a waiting game. The fish are constantly on the move looking for enough food to support the shoal. On the beach, many anglers use one or more rod rests because the rod is rather heavy. The best kind is one that keeps the rod tip high, where the line is held clear of the waves that turn over near to the sand or shingle. This irregular wave pattern can make bite detection difficult. With the rod high, positive bites are clearly seen.

Much of the productive cod fishing is undertaken on night tides, when the fish seem to come closer to the shore. Bite detection can be vastly improved by illuminating the rod tip with the aid of a torch or a Tilley lamp. The lamp will also give illumination when tying replacement rigs or baiting up. I tend to fish two rods, each with a glowing indicator. The gas-filled 'Isotope' kind are perfect as they do not require removal from the rod when casting. I've found that one needs two rods and their indicators to give a reference point. In the dark of the night, one bite indicator nodding by the pull of a fish can induce a kind of hypnotic effect over the angler as he gazes at the rod tip. But with two tips, the movement of one against the static position of the other is clearly seen to register a bite! Landing a heavy fish in a strong tide and inshore spoil can be a heart-stopping time. Gaffs are more trouble than they are worth. Bring the cod in steadily, always maintaining a tight line to the fish. With the casting leader grasped firmly in the hand, wait for a wave that floats the fish in toward you and beach the fish. A leader of 40 lb b.s. (18 kg) will let you drag the prize that short distance to get it clear of the waves. Most big fish lost gain their freedom just short of the shore, so make your fish-landing movements positive and unhurried.

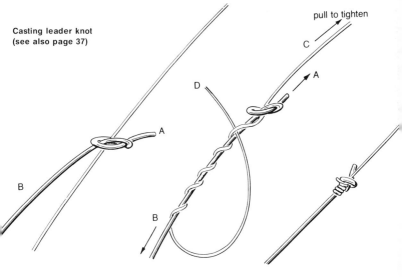

Casting leader knot
(see also page 37)

pull to tighten

C

A

D

A

B

B

(Below) *The tribod and sand spike, useful varieties of beach rod rest.*

Cod paternoster-leger combination trace

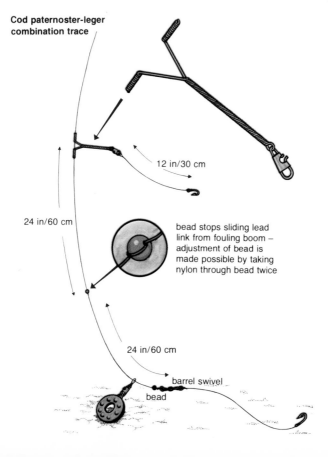

12 in/30 cm

24 in/60 cm

bead stops sliding lead link from fouling boom – adjustment of bead is made possible by taking nylon through bead twice

24 in/60 cm

barrel swivel

bead

Cod fishing from boats

Most sea fishing from boats is not species-selective. The baits and rigs that we use will handle a wide variety of fish. What we try to do is to be in the correct place, using fishing systems that will ensure attractiveness and positive hooking ability, for expected fish migratory movement. Cod fishing is little different from any other form of 'open ground' bottom fishing, but complications can arise with the varying sizes of the cod found. I like to get the most out of my fishing from a sporting point of view and endeavor to tailor the rod/line combination to match the fish that are available. This means using any one of three outfits, taking in one other factor and that is the angling environment. My gear works out something like this:

> 12 lb (5 kg) class line outfit using braided Terylene because of its non-stretch properties, for codling in light to average water conditions.

> 20 lb (9 kg) class gear for general cod fishing under all but the fiercest tidal conditions.

> 30 lb (13.5 kg) tackle for wreck fishing and where very big fish are expected in strong tide rips. If very large sinkers become necessary, I change to a wire line of the same breaking strain.

Heavier rod and line combinations would severely dampen the sensitivity of my fishing, and that is something I don't want.

Cod usually feed on the bottom and this trait determines the terminal rigs that we use. The paternoster rig is used at times of slack water only, but I do favour a paternoster/leger combination rig which gives the opportunity to put one bait on the seabed with another fluttering in the current about a foot above. The latter bait is often grabbed by smaller members of a shoal though its purpose is to be seen at distance. Fish moving over the seabed can smell *and* see the angler's offering. I set the height, above the bottom, of the boomed bait by adjusting the beads, between which the sinker can slide. When toothy species are expected— ling are always a possibility on broken cod ground—I form the hook links from pliant, cable-laid wire.

(Top left) *These late winter cod fell to pirks, artificial worms and flies fished over a wreck five miles (8km) out from Stonehaven, Scotland.* (Top right) *An artificial worm with a flexible tail, 'Mr Twister'.* (Left) *A cod paternoster/leger combination trace.*

The paternoster loses its purpose as the strength of tide builds. When this happens, I change to a legered presentation. One hook is all that is needed when fishing for good-size cod in a press of current. The rig can be of nylon or wire to suit expected fish, because cod aren't put off taking a bait that is mounted on a wire trace providing the rig isn't too stiff. When the tide is at its heaviest I find that the running leger doesn't, in fact, run at all! The angle formed by the nylon at the head of the Clement's boom is too acute. Over the years I've tried various variations of legering boom. Finally, this one has emerged. As tide puts a viscious bow in the reel line, it spreads the acute angle formed between two points 12 in (30 cm) apart. And the spring in the stainless steel wire from which the boom is made lets the two arms move together giving a little less friction to the pull of a taking fish.

Most open-ground cod fishing is done with worm or fish baits. There is nothing wrong with that thinking but there are times, over reef or wreck, when artificial lures come into their own. With a heavier density of fish living and feeding on live food, cod and other species will freely take a lure that has the action of a natural creature. Many anglers choose the metal pirk, which is jigged up and down to simulate a small fish. I prefer the plastic lures that need not be worked so vigorously because they have part of their attractiveness built in by the maker. Wiggling tails, such as are found on plastic sandeels and 'Mr Twisters' work beautifully in the slackest of water. Feathered lures also work perfectly, as the soft feather moves easily to look very much like tiny fish fry that would be found on the same holding ground.

Uptide casting techniques

I smile when I read of the newly discovered value of this fishing system! It is not new, and has been around in Europe for many years. On the East Anglian coast, where dinghy anglers until recently reigned supreme, we often cast uptide among the proliferation of sandbanks that litter our offshore waters. In the Baltic, German sea anglers have had to cast away from the charter boat for years; if they didn't, nothing would be caught. There are a number of reasons for the success of the technique; getting clear of the noise made by the boat's occupants, and the water disturbance made by the hull of the boat when moored in shallow water are clear benefits. So is the ability of a number of anglers to cover a greater area around the boat. Conventional boat fishing means that all of the baits are concentrated downtide of the boat. This is all right if the fish are swimming uptide in a tight shoal along the line of the baits but cod, to satisfy their appetites, spread over the feeding ground. Smell is often their only sense of a bait, the water is too murky for cod to see the

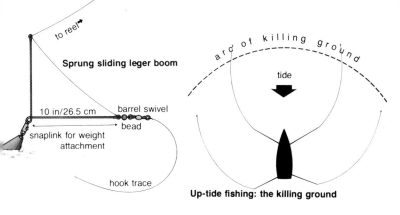

Sprung sliding leger boom

to reel

10 in/26.5 cm

barrel swivel

bead

snaplink for weight attachment

hook trace

arc of killing ground

tide

Up-tide fishing: the killing ground

(Above left) *The author's sprung sliding leger boom.* (Above right) *Baits should be positioned uptide and away from the boat to avoid the anchor rope.* (Below) *The basic sliding leger rig. It can be formed in nylon or flexible wire.* (Bottom) *The uptide casting rig must have a trace of manageable length to avoid casting problems.*

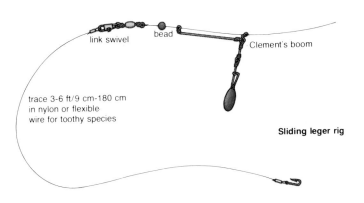

link swivel

bead

Clement's boom

trace 3-6 ft/9 cm-180 cm in nylon or flexible wire for toothy species

Sliding leger rig

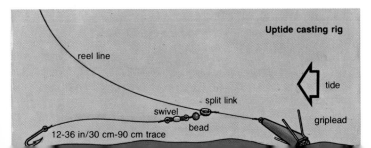

Uptide casting rig

reel line

tide

split link

swivel

bead

griplead

12-36 in/30 cm-90 cm trace

hook offerings. A wider spread of bait means that fish will spend longer in the area surrounding the boat.

If there is one drawback in the use of an uptide casting technique it is the danger of haphazard casting and lack of discipline displayed by boat fishermen who have had little casting experience. The rods, slightly shorter variants of a beachcaster, are used with casting multipliers. Luckily, those charter boat skippers who encourage this fishing style ensure that newcomers to uptide fishing follow their advice. Without doubt, the method is worth trying where cod, bass and other inshore migrants frequent the shallow, inshore fishing grounds.

Dab *Limanda limanda*

Dabs are widely distributed throughout the waters of Western Europe and up into the arctic zones. They prefer mud and sandy bottom in depths of up to 50 fathoms (100 m) but it is in shallow water, around the 20 fathom (37 m) mark that the bulk of fish are taken. This member of the plaice family can easily be recognized by rubbing the body from tail to head. The rough scales of the dab distinguish it from the plaice and flounder. There are no spots on the body and the lateral line has a sharp bend as it curves around the pectoral fin. Two pounds (1 kg) would be considered a specimen dab. They are rarely caught above 1 lb (0.45 kg) or so but the flesh is among the sweetest of our flatfishes. Their food consists of tiny crabs and small invertebrates. For dab fishing I like to use tiny ragworms and peeler crabs. The hermit crab is also a first rate hookbait with small particles of razorfish a close second.

Dabs have an extremely small mouth, so the baits and hooks have to be suited to this species. A long-shanked hook will give you a purchase when attempting to extract it. When I'm fishing from the shore into a known dab ground I use a simple nylon paternoster with two hooks. The lightest rod and line combination will handle the fish, subject to tidal conditions. From a boat, the 12 lb (5 kg) class outfit will give the sensitivity that allows perfect bite detection. This is important, for the dab bites very slowly, taking your worm in a progression of sharp jerks registered on the rod tip. One has to wait for the moment to strike. You must time the strike to make certain that the fish has the hook just within its mouth. Return undersized dabs to the water.

Use a leger rig, multi-hooked if you like, in even the slackest of current. This will let the fish pull the baits around, creating the seabed disturbance that encourages more flatfish to move towards the baits. I have taken dabs on the top hook of a paternoster tackle but I don't suggest that all dabs will rise in the tide to take a bait from this pattern of

Dab

Flatfish multi-hook rig

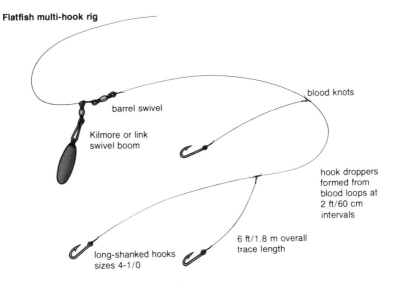

barrel swivel

Kilmore or link
swivel boom

blood knots

hook droppers
formed from
blood loops at
2 ft/60 cm
intervals

6 ft/1.8 m overall
trace length

long-shanked hooks
sizes 4-1/0

rig. Dabs congregate on the ground that suits their special needs. I can count the number of dab marks, offering fishing of certainty, on one hand around my part of the British coast though each of those marks provides the ultimate in light tackle fishing. In most cases dabs are caught accidentally on baits and rigs not intended for them—and on occasion when they have quietly whittled down a large bait before taking the hook into their mouths!

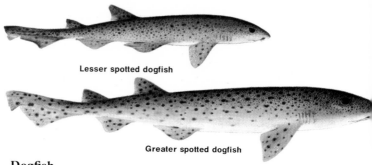

Lesser spotted dogfish

Greater spotted dogfish

Dogfish
Lesser spotted *Scyliorhinus caniculus*
Greater spotted *Scyliorhinus stellaris*

Both species of dogfish are found distributed throughout the angling waters of Western Europe. They swim at all depths but can be regarded as bottom feeding members of the shark family. Although cursed by the majority of sea anglers, the dogfish do provide sport on those occasions when the panfish seem to have disappeared! Separating the two species is easy, take a close look at their mouths. The nasal flap of the lesser spotted species appears as a single, unfrilled piece of skin whereas the greater spotted dogfish (or bull huss) displays a nasal flap with two frilled appendages (below). There are also differences in the position of the anal

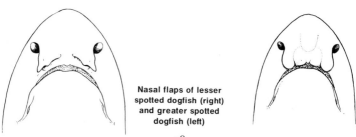

Nasal flaps of lesser spotted dogfish (right) and greater spotted dogfish (left)

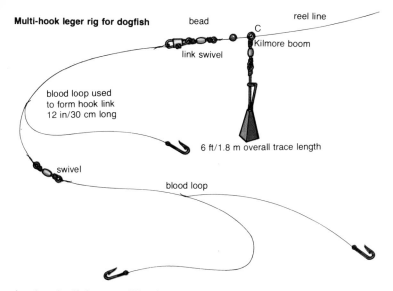

Multi-hook leger rig for dogfish

reel line

bead

C

Kilmore boom

link swivel

blood loop used
to form hook link
12 in/30 cm long

6 ft/1.8 m overall trace length

swivel

blood loop

*A nylon dogfish trace. Wire is not necessary, for these fish twist
wire into a badly kinked, tangled, good-for-nothing mess.*

fins. The lesser spotted's anal fin ends in front of the beginning of its
second dorsal fin. The anal fin of the bull huss ends halfway along
the second dorsal. Both species have very rough skin, resembling
the coarse grade of glasspaper. In both fish colour varies somewhat
subject to the habitat in which the fish live. Some dogfish are almost
totally black, indicating that they live in dark, rocky areas or places
with a predominance of heavy weed growth. Both species have spots
or blotches of dark brown colouring on a fawn background. The
lesser spotted's blotches are more regular than the huss markings, which
tend to be irregularly shaped. Both fish take live fish and scavenge for the
dead and sickly of the seas. The lesser spotted dogfish will also accept
worms and crustaceans as a hookbait. Most dogfish catches are
accidental for few sea anglers set out deliberately to hook these species.
Dogfish do not breed by haphazard spawning behaviour. The females
are fertilized internally and produce egg cases called 'Mermaid's
Purses' containing a single egg. The cases are attached to kelp fronds
and seaweed in shallow water, from which the tiny fish emerge within a
couple of months.
　　There are times when a catch of dogfish, notably the lesser spotted

variety, becomes important to the sea angler. This is when they would add valuable weight to a competition catch. Although they possess small teeth, with a sharp cutting edge, a wired terminal rig isn't really necessary. I tend to increase the gauge of nylon to allow for the damage done by hooking and playing these nuisances. Lesser spotted dogs move over open, sandy ground in small shoals, so a multi-hook rig becomes a valuable end tackle. One thing is necessary and that is a periodic inspection of the terminal gear, re-making the trace when signs of fraying, and subsequent weakening, appear. I prefer to offer small fish baits to this species on the basis that they worry a bait for a long time if it is too large for them to swallow. These false bites can be a nuisance, as there is a tendency to strike often without hooking the fish. Mackerel is the best bait as it has that essential ingredient—smell—by which dogfish track down their prey.

The bull huss is a larger, stronger fish that leads a solitary existence. Rarely do we find it swimming in shoals. A single-hook leger rig, wired if you are fishing in tope waters, will suffice. As the huss feeds in deep water, where other large species abound, the 30 lb (13.5 kg) class line rod and gear will be the correct choice. It is a pity that this fish is so often caught on heavy tackle because the captor then tells you that huss do not fight. But on light gear they are capable of a real fighting performance. Watch out for the lightly hooked huss! They have a nasty habit of holding the bait in their mouths and then letting themselves be winched up through the depths. On seeing the boat, the fish spits the bait back at the angler! The answer, if you think you are playing a huss, is to give a second, more vigorous strike to set the hook perfectly. Be careful when removing the hook from dogfish. If they wrap themselves around your arm, there will be no skin left on the tender underarm area. Restrain the fish properly before you attempt to unhook it.

When angling for dogfish, always tie a lask of mackerel onto the trace. When wire is used, the elasticated thread should wrap around between the ferrule and the eye of the hook.

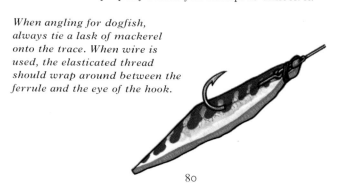

Eel *Anguilla anguilla*

At first sight, this species will appear to be a fish that deserves a place within the companion volume, on freshwater fishing, to this book, and so it does. But the freshwater eel is found in the sea. After growing in freshwater and before committing themselves to their nuptual journey to the Sargasso Sea in the North Atlantic, eels hang around the estuaries and inshore waters. As they feed and grow in the ponds and streams they turn yellow but as they drop to the sea there is a noticeable increase in silver along their flanks. The eel's eyes grow larger as maturity approaches. We cannot say with certainty what happens to the eel or conger eel after they embark on the spawning migration, for they aren't caught after leaving our shores.

Anguilla anguilla is caught at most places along the West Atlantic seaboard. This single species can be caught anywhere between Archangel and Gibraltar, so wide is its distribution. Almost any small particle of likely food will be taken by the eel. They cause inshore sea anglers a lot of grief by whittling down large baits intended for flounders or bass. Some anglers do actively fish for these sinewy creatures. After all, the flesh is highly regarded and is expensive when on a fishmonger's slab. To catch them, try a single or multi-hook rig using a paternostered lead. In streamy water the press of tide or outflowing river water will straighten the trace. Eels take time to get hold of the bait and do not move off with the offering. A leger tackle is unnecessary and only adds complication to the fishing.

Have a piece of coarse sacking handy when landing this fish. It is incredibly slimy, so the sacking allows you to grip the eel when removing the hook.

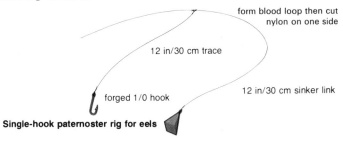

form blood loop then cut nylon on one side

12 in/30 cm trace

12 in/30 cm sinker link

forged 1/0 hook

Single-hook paternoster rig for eels

Conger eel *Conger conger*

The conger is altogether a different sea angling proposition to its freshwater cousin, for here is a fish of strength and ferocity! The conger eel begins life as a minute leaf-like creature, spawned in the mid-Atlantic depths. This planktonic animal then drifts on the ocean currents for years, undergoing a metamorphosis as it travels, to arrive off the coasts of Europe as a tiny, sinuous eel. As a juvenile, it lives and feeds among the rocky ground and kelpbeds of the littoral zone. As it grows, the eel seeks a habitat that can offer better feeding grounds to satisfy its appetite; offshore wrecks and foul ground give both food opportunities and hideaways from which to ambush lesser species. Some large congers remain in shallow water, using harbours and the cracks in breakwaters to provide a home and ground over which to scavenge.

Congers are fighters on rod and line. Not the sharp biting, fast-moving fish that makes the heart stop, but the powerful, tugging battler that pulls continuously against the strain of the rod. We fish for them with natural bait—lashes of mackerel, or whole fish, laid on the bottom with a legered trace that has a wired terminal section to the quality, forged hook. I use my 30 lb (13.5 kg) class rod and accessories for the

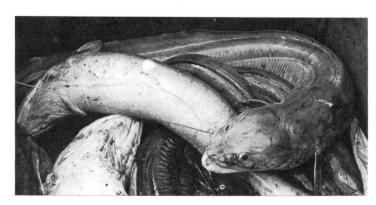

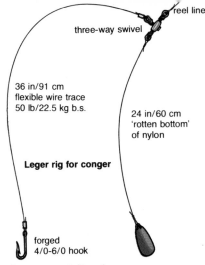

(Left) The fearsome, powerful conger. Large specimens have enormous strength. (Bottom left) The reefs and wrecks of Devon seas hold conger like this. (Right) There is no finesse in conger fishing rigs. The tackle must be strong enough to get the conger off the bottom and into midwater where the angler has a chance of getting it to the boat. Conger must be prevented from getting back to the bottom. Once wedged into a wreck or crevice, a large conger is probably lost to the angler.

reel line

three-way swivel

36 in/91 cm
flexible wire trace
50 lb/22.5 kg b.s.

24 in/60 cm
'rotten bottom'
of nylon

Leger rig for conger

forged
4/0-6/0 hook

average conger fishing but there are times, especially when out over a virgin wreck, when a 50 lb (22.5 kg) outfit is more suited to the tug of war that congering becomes. Essentially, tackle and knots must be the best, for here is one fish that will take you all the way in terms of strength.

The standard leger rig (see cod fishing) is perfect for fishing where the seabed is composed of lightly, broken ground. Where there are huge clumps of rock or the tangled super-structure of a wreck, I prefer to change to a long trace paternoster that incorporates a 'rotten bottom' link to the sinker. This link is only a connection, between the three-way swivel and the lead weight, of lower breaking strain nylon which will let you pull out from the foul ground if the lead becomes snagged, without losing your hooked fish! The running leger facility isn't required as it is not the intention to let the fish run into the safety of the wreck. As soon as a firm bite is registered, the conger must be hauled up a couple of fathoms to get its tail away from anything that it can be wrapped around. There is no doubt that a conger can and will attempt to do this. If it has, the result is a stalemate, for a bigger conger can stay attached to wreckage for long enough to reduce the angler to a quivering jelly.

Once the fish is in open water the fight becomes a progressive strain as the conger writhes and twists to throw the hook. Keep a steady pressure and recover line onto the reel. A skilled man, with a needle-sharp and stout gaff, is needed when at last the fish breaks surface. Don't give it an inch of slack line or let it begin that maniacal twisting that ruins traces and pulls the hook free from the conger's jaw.

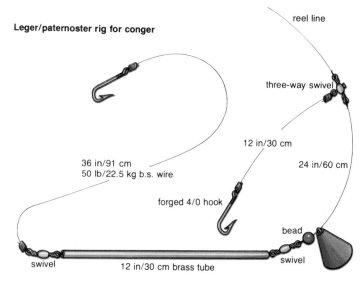

Leger/paternoster rig for conger

reel line

three-way swivel

12 in/30 cm

24 in/60 cm

36 in/91 cm
50 lb/22.5 kg b.s. wire

forged 4/0 hook

bead

swivel

swivel

12 in/30 cm brass tube

Reefs and sunken hulks produce the best of conger fishing but the inshore, broken ground will also provide sport with smaller specimens. The resident fish move over the bottom, roaming among the boulders where they probably rely on smell to find their food. The conger also possesses good eyesight, so I use a leger/paternoster combination rig in this habitat, offering baits that can be seen and smelt. The legered bait lies hard on the seabed with the boomed bait 2 ft (60 cm) up above the rocky bottom, just where congers can see it even if they are some distance away. The brass tube slipped onto the leger section of the rig is to keep one baited hook away from the other when lowering the rig quickly in a slack tide. I have found this rig a great aid when competition fishing where speed up and down is important. Knowing where conger are residing on a reef is vital to successful fishing. They aren't found all over a rocky environment but choose to lie at the base of

(Left) *When gaffing a conger, be positive! Do not allow the big eel to twist on the gaff—you will lose the fish.* (Below left) *A conger leger/paternoster rig with plenty of strength in all areas.*
(Below) *Once you have a conger in midwater it must be kept under constant rod pressure if it is to be beaten.*

The reef species

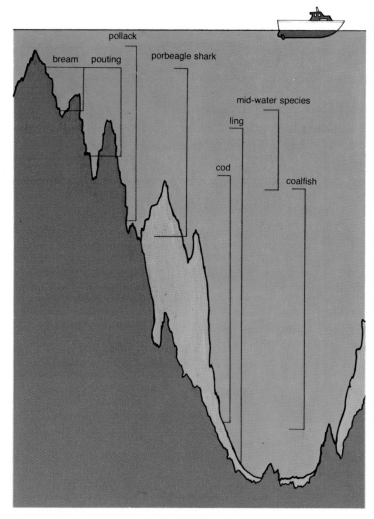

underwater cliffs where food will drift down to them in the shape of dead and wounded fish. My theoretical illustration gives some idea of where reef anglers can expect to encounter the various species that populate the pinnacles.

Conger from the shore

Shore fishermen need to step-up their tackle to meet the strength of the conger eel. A 12 ft (3.5 m) beachcaster, of 6–8 oz (170–225 g) capability, is needed on two counts; to handle the fight of the fish and to cast a reasonable-sized bait. A whole mackerel is not too big a bait for the conger of double-figure weight. I balance the rod to 18 lb (8 kg) nylon on a multiplying reel ending in a heavier-than-normal casting leader. This extra strength is so handy when landing a conger. It gives you something to grab hold of to drag the fish ashore. The gaff is your best landing aid from a pier or harbour wall, but on the open beach one simply walks the fish up on to dry land. Many shore conger fishers will favour the rocky ledges of our coastline. The fishing system is exactly the same. A biggish bait on a legered terminal rig. But the trouble starts when the played-out conger is breaking the surface! How can it be landed efficiently? The first essential is a long-handled gaff, one that can bend without breaking. This is the dodgy time when fishing for rock conger. The difficulty lies in your foothold not being as secure as one would enjoy on a harbour wall or hard sandy beach. It is a two-man operation which, incidentally, all rock fishing ought to be from the point of view of safety.

Don't attempt to remove hook traces from the mouth of a thrashing conger. Kill the fish humanely by a very heavy blow across the top of the head. Then leave it until you are sure that the specimen is dead—and even then take great care—before recovering the rig. It's a good idea to make up a number of the necessary traces before leaving home, so that fishing doesn't stop while traces are being recovered. If you have a big fish ashore and don't want to kill it, clip the wire trace off as close to the mouth as safety permits, then return the fish to its habitat to live and fight again. Many people will tell you that conger are not good eating. That is as maybe, but the flesh makes extraordinarily good soup!

(Left) *The distribution of fish over a pinnacle reef.* (Right) *A half-fish bait for conger fishing. As well as the tail, the forepart of the mackerel is equally effective with the hook through the gillcovers.*

Flounder *Platichthys flesus*

Possibly the most common flatfish of the north-east Atlantic, the flounder likes brackish water. The species has been found far up into the entirely freshwater regions of our major matchfishing rivers. They have even figured in a freshwater catch taken to the scales! Each late winter, the flounder migrates down to the sea. It spawns in the spring in shallow, inshore water where it gets trapped in the mesh of small trawlers. Soon after spawning the fish will move toward estuaries to feed on the rich life of the mudflats and creeks. It is then a fish that interests the sea angler. I wouldn't suggest that flounder are the gamest fighters but they can be relied on as residents of almost any rivermouth or creek that threads its way through the saltings.

The essential ingredient in flounder-fishing tackle is lightness, a delicacy in the hand that will transmit every tremor of a biting fish! I use a hollow glass pike rod for both casting a leger tackle and when there is the chance of float fishing at slack water. Here is one occasion when my fixed-spool reels come into their own, loaded with 10 lb line (4.5 kg). It may seem a little heavy but there is always the possibility of a good bass in the creeks, and I adopt a rolling leger technique for most of my floundering.

'Floundering' is an apt title, for the stickiness of the mud out on the estuary flats ensures that I have to take care where to go in the interest of safety. The clever way to plan a flounder fishing trip is to see the ground, over which you will trudge and fish, at dead low water. Register the channels in your mind so that the journey back, as the tide makes, will be an uneventful one! I like to begin my fishing soon after the first of the young flood tide. Flounders seem to swim with the new tide as it pushes against the freshwater flow from the land. This freshening brings out the invertebrate life from the mud to where the feeding flounders are cruising. The rig is of the simplest. Just an ounce (28 g) bullet lead rolling on the nylon, stopped by a barrel swivel. The hook is a long-shank 2 or 4 depending on the size and type of bait that I have been able to gather. If my luck was in, the slackwater period gave me time to dig a few worms and gather the odd peeler or soft crab—my favourite river mouth has a few rocky patches. Worms and crabs go in separate plastic bags that I can carry in my pocket. This is *roving* fishing, no need for a tackle box as one has to walk back from the sea ahead of the incoming tide that floods and fills the channels.

With the worm threaded over the hook and up onto the nylon, a cast should be made to the far side of the channel. Hold the rod tip fairly high

The main channel and subsidiary gullies that cross the sands of the Clogharne Estuary hold a concentration of thick, fleshy flounders. These flatties follow-up the incoming tides.

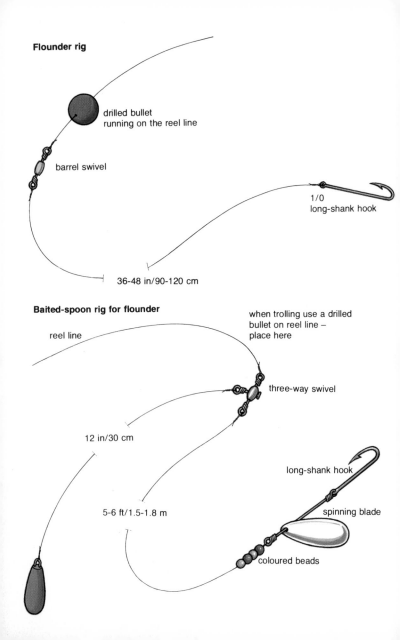

Flounder rig

drilled bullet
running on the reel line

barrel swivel

1/0
long-shank hook

36-48 in/90-120 cm

Baited-spoon rig for flounder

reel line

when trolling use a drilled
bullet on reel line –
place here

three-way swivel

12 in/30 cm

long-shank hook

spinning blade

5-6 ft/1.5-1.8 m

coloured beads

as the line swings round, following the rolling lead across the base of the creek. If the line stops and no plucking tremor is felt on the rod, lift the rod tip so that it clears the weed or lifts the lead from behind the empty shell that is trapping it. Sometimes a bite will follow the arrested lead, as a fish grabs the tail of the worm then pauses to swallow it. Make several casts from each place, fish are constantly moving with the tide. Then walk up-channel for 20 yd (18 m) or so before making further casts. Using this fishing style, you will be covering a lot of ground while keeping pace with the arrival of both tide and fish.

If a legered bait fails to catch a flounder, there is another proven method that could be adopted; the baited spoon. It is a wire mount on which a blade spinner is fixed so that it will whirl round in any sort of current. The worm bait, mounted on the long-shank hook, does not turn as the lure travels across the bottom. The idea is that flounders are attracted by the flashing blade sending up spurts of sand. Perhaps it looks like another flounder chasing the bait, which induces other fish to join the case. The rig can be cast from the side of a channel by adding a small bomb sinker on a short nylon link. Make the terminal trace at least 5–6 ft (1.5–2 m) long to keep it clear of the lead. The baited spoon rig works best when dragged behind a hardly moving dinghy being rowed slowly towards the approaching fish. I've found that the bites are severe wrenches, as the flounders have neither time to approach the bait carefully nor to take the worm casually.

The top of the tide, when high water gives a stand of slack and a calm comes to the estuary, is time to think of float fishing for flounder. It is the one flatfish that will freely rise up from the bottom to take a baited hook. Bait the rig with tiny ragworm or even slips of fresh mackerel. I know it sounds a doubtful bait for flatfish but it does chase fry and accept fishbait. The depth of water can be catered for by using a sliding float system (see wrasse) that can easily be adjusted to the tide as it begins to fall away. It is time to change back to the searching leger about an hour after high water.

(Above left) *The simple rolling leger rig is perfectly adequate for channel-dwelling flounders.* (Left) *The classic baited spoon rig for flounder fishing. The fluttering lure is probably taken for feeding fish.* (Right) *Solway Firth holds many good flounders.*

Gurnards
Grey *Eutrigla gurnardus*
Red *Aspitrigla cuculus*
Tub *Trigla lucerna*
Streaked *Trigloporus lastoviza*
Piper *Trigla lyra*
Lantern *Aspitrigla obscura*

Gurnards are a widely distributed group of marine fishes that appear fairly regularly in the catch of sea anglers. They are not specifically fished for, although the flesh is remarkably tasty. Two species, the piper and lantern, are deepwater fish whereas the other gurnards are found around most parts of the coastal plain.

Identification can be difficult, as there are subtle differences and the fish respond, in coloration, to habitat variation. In summary the differences are these:

> *Grey gurnard*, usually grey but can exhibit red hues.
> *Red*, bright red colour with a hardy discernible lateral line.
> *Tub*, pale red colouring with distinctive pectoral fins. The lateral line resembles a weal-like scar.
> *Streaked*, has a blunt head with streaked, vertical lines along the body and sometimes on the pectoral fins.
> *Piper*, has long spines projecting rearwards from the gillcases *and* forward facing spines projecting from the upper jaw.
> *Lantern*, has a series of large scales along the lateral line.

Gurnards feed on the seabed, where they will take practically any bait that they find. Most of my gurnards have come from broken ground where skate and conger were expected. These species demand big fish baits but the gurnards seem to be able to get to grips with a large mackerel lash. If you are lucky enough to find a gurnard hotspot, fish with long strips of fresh mackerel or herring.

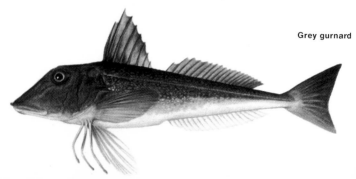

Grey gurnard

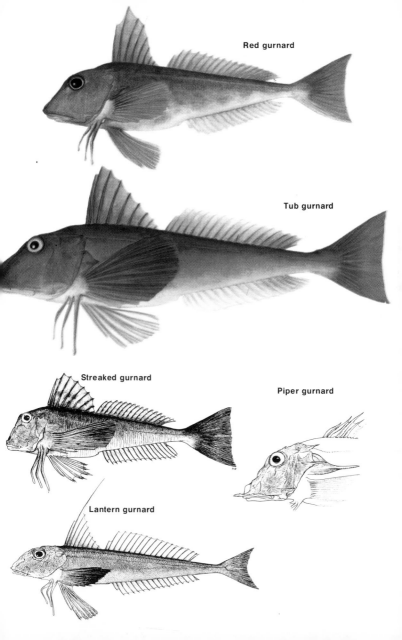

Red gurnard

Tub gurnard

Streaked gurnard

Piper gurnard

Lantern gurnard

Haddock *Melanogrammus aeglefinus*

This is a member of the cod family that can *really* fight. For its weight, the haddock is much stronger than the cod for it continues to fight when hooked and brought up from the depths, often full of strength when splashing around on the surface. Haddock are a coldwater species, preferring the more northerly waters of the Atlantic. They are clearly migratory, moving into established feeding grounds each season. This fish has three dorsal fins, a curved lateral line dark black in colour and an easily recognised black 'thumbprint' above the pectoral fin.

Most of our rod-caught haddock are taken in water up to 20 fathoms (37 m) deep over soft ground. A mixture of mud and sand gives ideal conditions for the colonial life of the haddock's food; worms, shellfish and small crustaceans such as shrimps and immature crabs. Haddock move out to their spawning grounds in much deeper water between the turn of the year and midsummer. Something like a hundred fathoms (180 m) appears to be the ideal depth for the annual breeding behaviour. Because of their preference for the soft ground, haddock are at the mercy of nearly every trawler and the species is in great danger of being fished out from the traditional waters around the British Isles. This is a pity, the fish fights well and is the tastiest of all the cod family.

Knowing the species' habits, we must find the suitable haddock environment before angling specifically for them. Luckily they are constant fish, returning year after year to exactly the same feeding grounds. Our tackle can be lightened to suit the average body weight that rarely exceeds 2–3 lb (approx. 1 kg) for the average specimen. What is important is the position of the hookbait relative to the rig and seabed. The haddock does not venture far from the bottom. So, our baits must be legered. For many years I had a real problem coming to terms with the delicate bite of this fish. Haddock have very soft mouths, from which I pulled the hook out too many times. A quick reaction to a bite was not desirable at all, an attitude entirely contrary to normal striking practice. The haddock needs to be given time to make its initial inspection of the bait and then to mouth it. I do not strike until there is a definite pull down on the rod tip, indicating that the fish has got a firm grip on the bait. To the newcomer to haddock fishing, this delayed reaction demands a lot of personal discipline. But, when mastered it pays dividends in the number of successful hookings.

Haddock are generally smaller than boat-caught cod, and have a

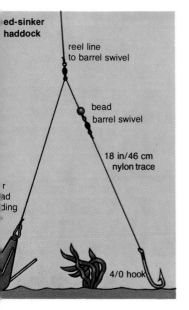

ed-sinker haddock

reel line to barrel swivel

bead
barrel swivel

18 in/46 cm nylon trace

r
ad
ding

4/0 hook

(Far left) The haddock, more a species for the hardy commercial fisherman than a sportfishing quarry. It is found mostly at depths of 20 fathoms (36m). (Far left, bottom) A haddock caught from a mark in the Firth of Clyde, the Pladda lighthouse. (Left) The haddock balanced-sinker rig. A tight line is kept by the angler from rod to terminal tackle, giving notice of the soft, mouthing bites typical of this species. The fish has to pull against the weight of the sinker. Used correctly, this rig prevents premature striking, a fault which loses the angler many fine haddock. Nothing is more annoying than 'bites' which are missed due to faulty technique.

smaller mouth. This suggests that baits ought to be matched to the haddock being caught. I use 4/0, needle-sharp hooks baited with a worm or shellfish, often presented as a cocktail of, say, lug and cockles or mussels. Only when fish strip is the bait do I go up to 6/0 hooks. It seems to me that although haddock will take fishbait, they feed more readily on something that tastes and smells of worm or shellfish.

Russ Russell, a rod craftsman from Redditch, Worcs, has played with the idea of matching a rod tip to the feeding style haddock. He has built in a quiver tip to a 12 lb (5 kg) class boat rod which is so sensitive that it gives a perfect indication of the arrival of a feeding fish and then lets the angler see and feel the progression of the bite. I know that this is a one-off fishing situation but there are many other shallow water feeding species that demand acute knowledge and reaction to what is happening below the boat.

This is one species that really only needs a single hook rig. If one complicates the terminal tackle with more than one hook, there can be trouble when more than one fish arrives in the feeding and baited area. They pull the baits around, mouthing slowly in a way that gives a series of false bites. A strike made too soon effectively pulls the bait away from the fish—and the angler is left with tattered baits. I've found that in very shallow water an uptide casting technique (see page 74) improves the bite/hook rate enormously, probably because the haddock hook themselves as they attempt to move away from the grip lead tethering the terminal gear uptide of the dinghy. Finally, haddock are not as well able to reproduce themselves as cod. The female fish spawn far fewer eggs and the natural predation on them is high. Take only the fish that you need in the late winter. One gravid female returned could mean a lot of fish for anglers in a few more years.

Mackerel *Scomber scombrus*
Garfish *Belone belone*

I bring these two species together as they are so often found swimming alongside one another in nature. The annual migration of mackerel shoals, from deepwater off the south-west of Britain, appears to match the arrival of the garfish in the months of July and August. Both species can be regarded as offering the gamest of sport fishing, providing the angler's tackle is matched to the fishing ability of these small fish. Too often the mackerel is only thought of as a bait fish to be feathered out of existence!

Until recently it was not fully understood what happened to the vast shoals of mackerel during the winter months. Now, the actions of British

Mackerel

Garfish

Feather rig for mackerel

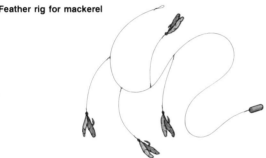

Mackerel feathers. When dry, just feathers, but in the water they adopt a look and action that resemble a small shoal of fry.

trawlers and Russian factory ships have changed our theories. Early writers assumed that mackerel went far out from our shores into deepwater. Now we know that they do not venture far from the coast and are critically vunerable to the massive predation methods that the greedy commercial interests have developed so successfully. Sea anglers now realize that the commercial winter predation has resulted in a breakup of the summer shoals. Where a few minutes' concentrated feathering once gave more than enough bait for the day, we can now struggle for hours to get barely enough. And sometimes we fail to find a single mackerel.

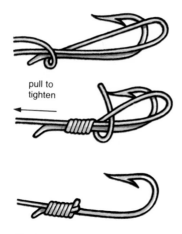

pull to tighten

(Left) *Use the whipping knot to tie your own mackerel feathers. Chicken hackles are attached to spade-end hooks.* (Right) *A traditional trolling spinner and tiny rubber sandeels are attractive to shoaling mackerel.* (Below right) *Take great care when swinging in a string of mackerel. The wildly wriggling fish and accompanying hooks can cause nasty injuries to nearby anglers. Care must also be taken when removing the fish from the hooks. Remember, too, to kill the mackerel quickly.*

Both mackerel and garfish are pelagic species. They exist by harrying shoals of immature fish of many species. This feeding pattern demands that they travel constantly to satisfy the shoal's appetite. Our feathers or single, sporting, baits must simulate fry if they are to prove efficient fish catchers. When using a feather trace to bring something useful to the baitbox, I make certain that the feathers are at their most effective by trimming the feather so as to leave just a few millimetres protruding beyond the bend of the hook. Many commercially dressed traces leave the feathers an inch (2.5 cm) or more beyond the hook, and mackerel grab the feather without getting the hook! The modern style of trace, involving the use of three or more plastic dressings sometimes interspersed with a flashing metal attractor, can and does catch mackerel when they arrive in a shoal. I still prefer the feathers however, as they carry down and release pockets of air that have become trapped within the feathers. Perhaps the bubbles attract the fish more effectively.

I regard the mackerel as one of the sea's most colourful fighters. Take a light spinning rod, 5 lb (2 kg) line and a tiny blade spinner or spoon on any mid-summer boat-fishing trip and you will enjoy a sport that is hard to better! Related to the oceanic tunny, the mackerel is built for speed. When hooked, mackerel dash around making long, stripping runs that will easily take 50 yd (46 m) of line off the spool. I set my fixed-spool drag with little pressure and apply drag with a finger on the rim of the spool. If there is a problem in this kind of mackerel fishing it is that your fellow anglers in the boat will not like the antics you are forced to engage in to

keep contact with the speedy one! Probably, the dinghy angler gets the best of this light tackle fishing. With only one or two anglers in a boat, control of the fish is easier and the experiences are more closely shared.

Garfish will also chase a spinner through the waves. When hooked, they cartwheel as they are played on a light line. The species speeds around the outside of the mackerel shoals that are normally slightly deeper in the water. With a calm sea float fishing becomes a proposition from the boat or at the shoreline. A light float set-up, using a No. 8 hook baited with minute slips of mackerel strip, will give indication of a bite while supporting the bait in the upper layers of the warm water. Keep the bait very small, for hidden away under the elongated upper bill, is a tiny mouth that cannot take in mackerel-sized baits. When playing garfish, a tight line is essential. Their movements are always energetic and the fish has an ability to throw the hook very easily. Return the gars to the sea if you cannot face eating something that has green bones. The flesh is quite sweet-tasting but the culinary value diminishes when your relatives view the body on the plate!

(Right) *The oily flesh of a fresh mackerel is probably the most killing bait in all sea fishing. Here it is being cut into thin lashes, or lasks. (Below) A garfish float rig. The fast-swimming garfish can be detected when it bites as the float changes position in the water from the vertical to the horizontal. On light tackle, a hooked garfish gives an entertaining struggle.*

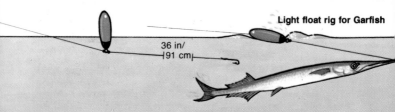

Light float rig for Garfish

36 in/
91 cm

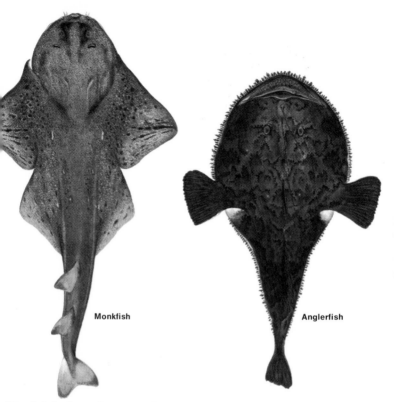

Monkfish

Anglerfish

Monkfish *Squatina squatina*
Anglerfish *Lophius piscatorius*

Half shark and half skate, the monkfish is an unlovely specimen which inhabits the same ground that we associate with the ray family. A prehistoric reminder, perhaps, something that has evolved between these species? In reality, the monkfish is closer to the sharks as it possesses pectoral fins that are not joined to the head of the fish. In the skate and ray families, the pectoral fins have become extensions of the body. The mouth is positioned right up front on the fish's head, not underneath and back from the head as would be expected from the other two groups. Monkfish are confused with the anglerfish which has a shape roughly the same. The major difference is internal. The monk is a cartilagenous fish, which means that it has a gristly skeleton, whereas

A monkfish from Tralee Bay, Ireland, which put up a fight like a salmon. Such a struggle is very unusual in the monkfish, which usually comes to the boat like a sack of potatoes. The species is in danger and all specimens should be returned.

anglerfish have the true bony-skeleton. The latter species has a huge mouth, full of sharp teeth and its own fishing lure! This is a waving, modified first dorsal fin that acts as an attractor to draw small fish toward the angler's mouth.

Neither species can be said to put up the best fight in the sea angling world. The monk, growing to big weights—60 lb (27 kg) is not impossible—can be winched in with the same thrill as playing a huge clump of seaweed. Bulk it has, but no gameness! The anglerfish's only claim to fame is that the one we catch is our glimpse of the type of fish that swims in the deeps of our oceans and seas. Scientific expeditions, using deepwater trawling methods and submarine vehicles, have proved that there are all manner of anglerfish and similar 'swimming mouths' to be found in the total darkness of the vast depths. We shall never catch or see but a minute number of these marine wonders.

Mullet
Thick-lipped grey *Chelon labrosus* (illustrated above)
Thin-lipped grey *Liza ramada*
Golden-grey *Liza aurata*

This is a group of shoreline species that can be regarded as one as the techniques and baits are identical for all of them. These pelagic fish migrate into North Atlantic waters during the summer months, feeding on plankton and grazing over the estuarine mudflats. Mullet are powerful fish that will test the tackle and ability of any shore angler. Ideally, one needs strong tackle but mullet are both hook-shy and finicky in their feeding habits, which means that if you want to catch them you will have to fish light and skilfully. Mullet, like flounders, can be found feeding well up-river beyond the tidal influence. It is stated that the thin-lipped species can tolerate a totally freshwater environment. This is borne out by the number of land-locked shoals that only return to the salty habitat when a gale or extremely high tide floods over into the freshwater lake. They are also said to be able to live in water that is virtually stagnant, breathing air by raising their mouths above the water's surface. I haven't seen this behaviour although I have come across mullet that were trapped in very shallow water from which they would be lucky to escape easily. I imagine that hot weather, combined with evaporation, would diminish the oxygen supply rapidly.

Flounders and mullet have a regular migratory route in and out of bays, inlets and estuaries, seemingly dictated by the movement of the tide. Each day, at the same phase, the fish will move in to feed. It is this regularity that gets them caught. The expert mullet fisher is a determined man who quietly observes his fish, coming to know a good deal about their lifestyle. A lot of effort is given to ground-baiting, a process of gradual introduction to feed that can be put on a hook, for the mullet's natural food is too small to use as a bait. Diatoms and algae cannot be used by the fisherman. But if you feed soaked bread downtide for a period of time the fish will investigate. In harbours, below seaside piers and at drainage outfalls, we find a different situation. The mullet

Mullet identification

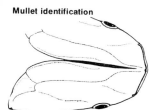

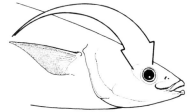

Thick-lipped grey (above) has narrow 'throat' on underside of head. Thin-lipped (below) has wide 'throat'.

Pectoral fin of golden-grey (above) when folded forward reaches eye, unlike thin-lipped grey (below).

are conditioned to the acceptance of a vast array of food particles. They expect a variety of edible matter to be thrown, drifted or swept to them. In these fishing places a less delicate approach can be the order of the day. One can see mullet taken on fairly heavy tackle on strips of fish bait. The thick and thin-lipped mullet combine their feeding habits to strictly timed patrols, governed by tidal movements. It is all a question of habit, as the fish come to scavenge at defined marks.

I like trotting small ragworms down the tide on light float tackle. This style of fishing can take place in any smooth tidal flow where wind and freedom from obstructions give a clear passage to the tackle. The rig is simple. An Avon float carrying a heavy shot load near to the hook takes the bait down quickly in fastish flow. In slack water, I like to adopt an antenna float system. The float is locked, at depth, with swan shots. The rest of the loading is carried at midpoint on the trace. This has the advantage of presenting a slow-dropping bait that free-falls through the current and attracts the mullet. Using my 10 ft (3 m) carp rod and an 8 lb b.s. (3.5 kg) line, to counteract the wild fight of this species in shallow water, I have the control necessary to keep the tackle trotting correctly. Use the sharpest, forged size 4 hook you can obtain. It will accommodate a small worm without too much of the iron showing yet hold the fish.

There is no reason why a paternostered rig should not be used when mullet fishing. The tackle make-up must be fine so that the fish are not put off by too many bits of ironmongery. The method suits a busy harbour where fish are not scary but there is a lot of turbulence from boats that would knock a float tackle around. My choice for a harbour mullet, and those that patrol along the rocky ledges, is a freelined bait, cast out with just a nipped-on split shot to fall freely through the surface film. Surface bites are seen as the fish open their mouths to swallow the offering. The old timers always advised us to strike as soon as we saw the white, rubbery lips open. They said that by the time a strike was made, the fish would have closed its mouth over the bait—such is the speed of a mullet take! Of course, freelining is a constant casting and retrieving method but it can be exciting. Keep the drag setting on your reel fairly loose. Mullet can move fast when hooked so be prepared for initial long runs that taper off only gradually. Knots are important. Take the reel line right through to the hook, with just one tucked half-blood tied properly.

(Left) *A typical mullet habitat with channels winding between sand and mudbanks at low tide. Weed and rocks are covered at high tide.* (Below) *Two float-fishing rigs for the wary mullet.*

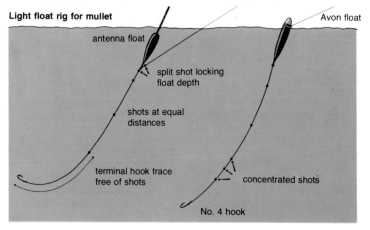

Light float rig for mullet

Avon float

antenna float

split shot locking float depth

shots at equal distances

terminal hook trace free of shots

concentrated shots

No. 4 hook

Red mullet

There is another fish, the red mullet, *Mullus surmuletus*, that boat fishermen catch occasionally. It is a deepwater fish that favours a broken ground habitat. Unrelated to the true mullets, this species is not fished for specifically but makes a superb meal. It frequents the south and western coasts of the British Isles and down through the Bay of Biscay.

Plaice *Pleuronectes platessa*

A prize catch for both sea anglers and the commercial operator, the plaice is under threat because of the continuing demand for its delicate flesh. Plaice are a widely distributed species and will frequent the offshore sands of the shallow coastal waters anywhere between the Bay of Biscay and North Cape. Expect to find this flatfish wherever tidal conditions allow a colony of mussel or other shellfish to become established. Plaice are shoal fish, where you hook one you'll find others feeding. They do not enter into estuaries in the same way as flounders do, but can be expected to haunt the same offshore habitat during the winter months. Some anglers find difficulty in separating the two fish. Both species will display spots of orange colour, but those of the plaice are more brilliant. The simplest identification factor is that plaice have a row of hard, bony nodules on the head behind the eyes. They lack the two rows of bony scales that the flounder displays at the base of both anal and dorsal fins.

The plaice spawns in spring, soon after the hard frosts disappear. Female fish lay many thousands of eggs in water of around 20 fathoms (37 m). After hatching, the larval plaice seek the shallow water over sand and muddy shores. They can be found in the seapools of most holiday beaches. Perfect replicas of the adult fish, the tiny plaice fry are at risk from the fish-eating seabirds that scavenge after every high tide. There is a lot of evidence to suggest that plaice feed best in calm sea conditions. This behaviour is perhaps due to the fish's need to see clearly. Any inshore disturbance, such as from a pounding wave pattern, will raise clouds of sand that severely reduce the vision of the feeding fish. It may well be, therefore, that a high sand content in the water affects the behaviour of the shellfish that the plaice is preying upon. Whatever brings the plaice in to feed on the shellbeds, they can be expected to provide useful sport from Easter onwards. Having recovered from the rigours of spawning, the fish feed avidly. About 5 fathoms (9 m) of water seems to be the average depth at which they establish residence. They are also found in areas populated with feeding crabs and this causes a nuisance to anglers as they find their baited hooks constantly stripped by the attentions of the ever-hungry crustaceans. Crabs are faster moving to the bait, stealing in before the fish can mouth the offering. A way in which to defeat the crabs' attentions is to use a slightly buoyant rig, one that will keep the bait just off the seabed. Plaice will rise a short distance in the water to grab a worm or shellfish cocktail hookbait. The required buoyancy can be achieved by sliding a bored cork on to the legered trace about 12 in (30 cm) from the hook.

A flatfish species that is under tremendous pressure from angling and commercial trawling, plaice are becoming difficult to find in numbers. These flatties were caught from Portpatrick offshore marks. Another good plaice mark is Deal, on the Kent coast.

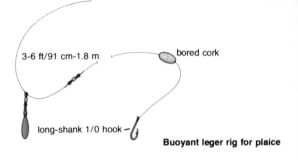

3-6 ft/91 cm-1.8 m | bored cork

long-shank 1/0 hook

Buoyant leger rig for plaice

Legering must be the correct style for plaice fishing as the fish feeds hard on the bottom and takes the bait fairly slowly. The bite is felt as a number of jerks to the rod tip. Your reaction to this must be cautious. Keeping a tight line between rod and fish will help in establishing when to strike. Wait for a positive pressure on the line that says the fish has taken the bait into its mouth. Strike against the tight line with a firm lift. No exaggerated over-the-shoulder sweeps are necessary, it will only pull the hook from the fish's mouth. A leger rig can be tied up with two or three hooks on the premise that more than one fish will be in the immediate vicinity of your bait. Tie your hooks on with a tucked half-blood knot, leaving a whisker of nylon jutting out from the knot. This will stop the threaded worm from pulling down to the hookbend. Plaice, like other flatfish, are adept at stripping the worm without getting the hook firmly into their jaws.

(Above) *A buoyant leger rig with the bait suspended over the bed by cork. This tends to prevent crabs from stealing the bait.* (Left) *Plaice put up a good struggle on light tackle. Their bite is similar to all flatties and indicates their feeding habit. Never gaff them, for it spoils the tasty flesh.* (Right) *Pollack fishing from a dinghy under the lee of the Holy Isle in the Firth of Clyde, Scotland. This mark is a superb one for reef fish and continues to provide anglers with tremendous sport.*

Pollack *Pollachius pollachius*

If there were prizes for the quality of fighting, the pollack would figure
very high on the list. For the angler, pollack fall into two classes: those
found off a rocky shore; and the much larger fish that inhabit reefs and
wrecks. This is a fish of the west; it is found from the coast of Portugal,
up around the British Isles and into the arctic regions of Norway. Unlike
its near relative the coalfish, the pollack is not a deepwater species and
favours the inshore waters high on the Continental Shelf.

The fish is greenish-black in body colour with a pronounced lower
bottom jaw. The lateral line is marbled black and slightly curved over
the pectoral fin. Juvenile fish stay close to the kelp of the reefy shoreline
where they adopt a reddish hue, similar to the general colour of their
weedy habitat. To the angler, pollack are a fish of summer. In winter

they depart to much deeper waters and they spawn in February to May. This fish is a live-fish feeder. Because of this trait it has become a sporting species, hooked by the angler on a wide variety of artificial baits and spun lures.

Pollack from the shore

Pollack are fond of the broken ground around the base of cliffs and rocky ledges. They hide within the kelp fringes from where they are able to ambush other shore-dwelling species. Two angling systems are in order: spinning in all its forms, and float fishing a strip of natural bait. Spinning baits can be artificial lures made of metal, which have casting weight built-in to them, or plastic lures that resemble something in nature. Sandeels, made to wiggle attractively, are a favourite among spinfishers. I also employ natural baits, prawns, strips of fish, whole fish, such as whitebait and sprats, worked on a baitcasting rig by casting out and varying the rate of retrieve to give the terminal tackle a semblance of reality. To be successful, this fishing method has to be a continuous process of casting and working back. It is not a technique for the lazy angler. There is little fish-catching potential in a lump of fish that is cast and wound back with no thought of putting life into it.

Spinning with artificials is quite another matter! The maker has done his best to put action into the bait. Metal spoons have an undulating swerve through the waves that attracts fish. Rubber sandeels, popular because they look like the real thing, have a tail into which has been designed a vane that makes the thing wiggle or vibrate rapidly—a certain fish-taker when shoals of fry are about. The 'Mr Twister' bait (see cod) is another artificial that works splendidly on pollack. The plastic worm/wriggler has to be fitted with a weighted jighead that provides enough casting weight to get the jig down to waiting fish.

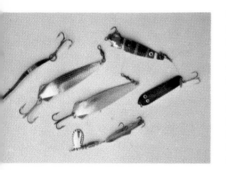

(Left) *Pollack will chase metal spoons greedily, particularly when the lures simulate the colour and action of fish fry.*
(Right) *Cut thin lasks from a mackerel, ensuring that some of the silvery belly skin is left to glisten in the water.*
(Far right) *This lure can be trolled or cast from the shore with the aid of a jighead that weights the artificial worm.*

Pollack caught from the shore aren't really big fish. One of 6 lb (3 kg) would be called a specimen. But what they lack in size is made up for in that first, heart-stopping wrench and drive down into the kelp. A fish that is allowed to get among the tangle is generally lost to the angler. On their initial run, pollack have to be held, then powered out from the security they are heading for. The pollack is in a winning position where kelp comes almost up to the surface. Any slack line during the fight or lack of concentration when bringing the beaten fish to the surface can be hazardous. Floatfishing can provide great fun while keeping the pollack farther out during the fight, away from the kelp margins. The bait can be suspended quite near to the surface well out from the shore. Notice of a biting fish is clearly seen by the actions of the float. Although the fish makes every attempt to gain the haven of weeds, I've found that the float helps in keeping the fight offshore in the clear water.

Fishing with a float at distance can produce one problem—that of securing a perfect hookhold on the strike. The amount of line to pick up off the water, coupled with friction where the line passes through the float, reduces the power of the strike at the hook. Use a sensible nylon breaking strain, one of about 8–10 lb (3.5–4.5 kg), to reduce the elasticity found in lighter line. Friction, which absorbs striking force at the float, can be overcome somewhat by attaching the float at one point only. Line that passes through a plastic tube within the body of the float vastly reduces the strike applied by the rod.

I find that at least a 10 ft (3 m) rod is required to cope with the casting, strike and problems of controlling a fish from a rock ledge. A firm foothold is essential to aid effective use of the tackle to subdue your fish. Landing the pollack, or any other fish caught from this kind of situation, is best achieved with a landing net. Gaffs are unnecessary as there are

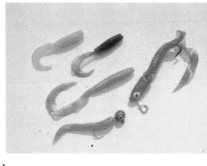

few times when the fish needs to be killed. Ensure that the net is large enough and has a handle that reaches the water's edge.

Pollack from a boat

This species is one that can be trolled for. Using a dinghy, the lure can be trailed behind with just enough forward motion to provide steerage way yet keeping the bait fairly high in the water. Pollack will dash out from the kelp to take the same lures that the shore angler might be casting. The fish do not seem to mind the vibrations of a slow-running outboard engine. I find that 40 yd (36 m) or so is enough distance between lure and boat to overcome the fish's natural fear. A small lead, which can be a spiral or drilled bullet, provides enough weight to get the lure below the wave pattern where it can swim with the correct action. Some anglers regard trolling as a chuck-it-and-chance-it technique, requiring little skill on the angler's part. This is nonsense, for the skill lies in understanding the fish's life style, knowing where it will be, then adjusting the speed of troll to get the lure down to the predator.

Float rig for pollack

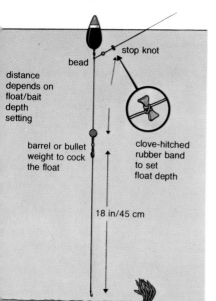

distance
depends on
float/bait
depth
setting

bead

stop knot

barrel or bullet
weight to cock
the float

clove-hitched
rubber band
to set
float depth

18 in/45 cm

(Left) *Float-fishing for pollack can be very rewarding.* (Below) *When pollack fishing, carry a selection of rubber eels in various sizes and colours to match the habitat and mood of the fish.* (Below right) *On the strike, friction must always be avoided when float-fishing at a distance.*

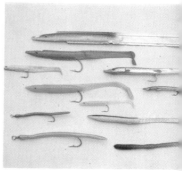

Spinning can be productive when the dinghy is moored or drifted 30 yd/m or so off the cliff face. Spinning into the kelp means that fish are fought away from the hazards, from the tangle toward the boat that rides in open water. Spinning should be slower over the ground. With the bait allowed to fish lower in the water, clear of the shoreline of weeds, fishing is more effective and a greater depth and coverage are achieved. On a safety theme, watch the conditions closely as a rockbound lee shore is not the place to have engine trouble! Keep a weather eye open for those subtle changes of wind and water that warn an experienced boatman to get away before the sea spells trouble. Always assume that worsening weather will continue to deteriorate, so don't take chances!

Deepwater pollack fishing

Wreck and reef fishing tackles and lures are not selective, in that the methods used will take a variety of resident fish found on this habitat. Ling, coalfish, cod and pollack will greedily grab the same bait. Because of this, we tend to wire the traces, expecting that ling will happen along and their razor sharp teeth determine the terminal rig to use. Pollack, and the other denizens of the wreck, are not tackle shy. It is probably true to say that any wreckfish that has seen an angler's trace up close was caught. So they don't live to spread the word about us and our rigs! In deepwater, the 20 lb (9 kg) class outfit will give the quality of sport of which wreck and reef pollack are capable. The fight isn't at all like that put up by the shore-dwelling fish. Deepwater pollack take a bait hard, fight like blazes for the first few fathoms then quieten rapidly as the pressure change affects their bodies. A pity really, as the larger specimens are enormously powerful when they make that first, crashing rod-bending dive down to the safety of the deeps.

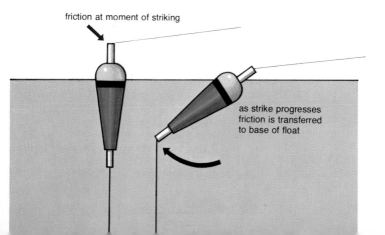

friction at moment of striking

as strike progresses friction is transferred to base of float

Pouting *Trisopterus luscus*

A small member of the cod family held in little esteem by sea anglers, the pouting does bring the sport of sea angling to a lot of people. Its tugging bites, as the fish steals the hookbait intended for bigger, more attractive species, has caused many an angler to cease his fishing for the day. If we view sea fishing as sport and not always as a way of augmenting the contents of the deepfreeze, this little fish does have a value. Its distribution is more southerly than all of the other members of the cod family. Pouting are not found in great numbers above the Yorkshire coast or beyond the Solway Firth. The species favours rough ground, where a mixture of rock and weeds provides an ideal habitat for the grazing of this small shoal fish. Pouting can also be sure to lurk around the piling of pier structures, where marine growths provide a profusion of the small creatures that pouting feed on. Over deeper water, in the vicinity of wreck and reef, this fish will be caught if a small bait is fished in mid-water, above the bulk of the rising structure. There is a similarity in feeding level and behaviour to the sea breams.

Fish small worm or shellfish baits for pouting on hooks of 1/0 size. Too large bait will result in tweaking pulls by the fish as it struggles to nibble the bait down to swallowing proportions. Pouting will take tiny slips of fresh fish used as hookbaits, or you can offer them paternostered baits because pouting swim above the seabed. A floatfishing style can be adopted when fishing from the harbour wall or jetty that juts out into a broken-ground bottom. The species reacts to groundbaiting with mashed fish offal drifted down the tide.

The Rays

These are one of the most important groups of marine fish. They provide the commercial industry with a large part of their catch and at least two of them, the thornback and blonde ray, give sport to many anglers. Although closely allied to the true skate, fishermen tend to put them into a sporting category apart from the heavy strain that forms the fight when large comman skate are the quarry. All of the rays can be handled on light or medium class tackle. Some venture close to the shoreline and there are a couple of species that we rarely see, as they are confined to the deeper waters.

Thornback ray   Blonde ray

Thornback ray *Raja clavata*
Blonde ray *R. brachyura*

The thornback ray exhibits a varying degree of coloration, but generally the base hue is a dirty grey. The fish has 'thorns', from which it gets its name, along the ridge that forms the central spine of the flattened body and patches on the wings. This is our commonest ray, favouring shallow water where it preys upon small fish, worms and crustaceans. Thornbacks can grow to weights of about 20 lb (9 kg), this size and the fact that

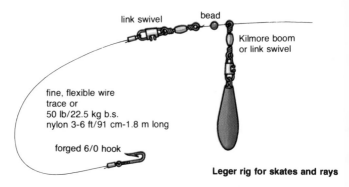

link swivel   bead

Kilmore boom
or link swivel

fine, flexible wire
trace or
50 lb/22.5 kg b.s.
nylon 3-6 ft/91 cm-1.8 m long

forged 6/0 hook

Leger rig for skates and rays

they possess strong, crushing teeth call for terminal rigs that can cope
with the species. Many anglers construct a leger rig that incorporates a
trace of flexible wire. This is a sound idea where fish are expected to be
large but the use of wire may well cut down the number of potential
strikes. From the shore I now use a heavy gauge nylon hook trace. Line of
50 lb b.s. (22.5 kg) handles the fish *and* those fierce teeth adequately. Ray
fishing from a boat gives the opportunity for other species, notably tope,
to take the bait. On these occasions I believe that a wired terminal trace
is a worthwhile system to adopt.

Detecting the bite and moment to strike home the hook can present
difficulties to the angler unaccustomed to catching rays. The fish does not
dart in to grab a bait. Its arrival is slow, almost ponderous. The fish
sights the bait, moves over it to position the mouth above the offering,
then flops gently onto the seabed. Attention to the rod tip will show the

(Above) *Nothing complicated
about this simple running leger
rig for ray fishing.* (Left) *Three
fish on one trace here—two
lesser spotted dogfish and a
thornback ray. They fell to Neil
McLean, who was fishing in
the Tylers International
Championship.* (Right) *The
spotted ray is one of the smaller
members of its group of fishes.
It lives in moderately deep water
over sandy or rough ground.*

arrival of a ray as a pronounced dip in the rod followed by a period when nothing happens. The ray is positioning itself and mouthing the bait. If the strike is made too early, the fish will not have the bait in its thick rubbery jaws. All we do is drag the rig from under the ray. This sudden movement will also cause the fish to leave the bait alone. Hold the rod, tighten the line to take in all the slack and wait for a pull which shows that the thornie is beginning to move off. Then give a lusty over-the-shoulder strike that will overcome line elasticity and set the hook firmly in the tough jaw. Be prepared for a fight, for while rays aren't speedy fighters they can give a protracted battle in any run of tide.

The thornback ray will lie low in the strongest phase of the tide. When the water slackens the fish will emerge from the seabed, where it hides from the strong flow by digging into the mud or sand, and then quarters the open ground searching for food. Sandbanks are a favoured habitat. The fish roams the surrounding gullies and channels, avoiding the top of the submerged sands where the tide is strongest and the habitants fleet of fin.

The blonde is the largest of this group of rays. Found more to the south and west of the British Isles, the species lives over similar ground and shares the feeding habits of the thornback ray. Blondes do not seem to come inshore in very shallow water. They prefer the channels and offshore sandbanks in water over 10 fathoms (18 m) deep. Identification is slightly confusing as the spotted, or homelyn ray, *R. montagui*, looks very similar. The blonde ray is a sandy-yellow base colour with dark spots that cover the entire body out to the very edge of the wing margins. Spotted rays do not grow to large sizes, 6 lb (3 kg) would be a large fish. Its spots do not extend to the wings and on the top of each wing it has a

Spotted ray

Cuckoo ray　　　　　　　　　　　**Sandy ray**

single, light-coloured patch surrounded by darker markings.

Two other ray species have spots on their wings. The cuckoo ray *R. naevus* has a distinctive, chocolate circle on each wing which is picked out with white wavy streaks. In deeper water we find the sandy ray, *R. circularis*. Much darker, the fish displays a number of clear spots, yellow or pure white, on each wing. To the west of our shores, in Atlantic waters, two more rays are found. Both have wavy lines and stripes across the upper colouring of their bodies. The small-eyed ray, *R. microocellata,* often described as the painted ray, shows pale wavy lines on a background of muted yellow. Within the same sea area, the undulate ray, *R. undulata*, appears. Its body colour is a drab brown broken by dark brown, almost black, striations.

In the North Sea, particularly in areas of inshore sandbanks, we find the stingray, *Dasyatis pastinaca*. This is a dangerous fish if handled carelessly. On the whip-like tail there is a sharp, poisonous spur which can cause a nasty wound that has a paralyzing effect and is extremely painful. The fish comes close in to sandy beaches, where it may well take a bait intended for thornback rays. The stingray is a heavy fish that can fight and is always attractive to beach fishermen, but is dangerous.

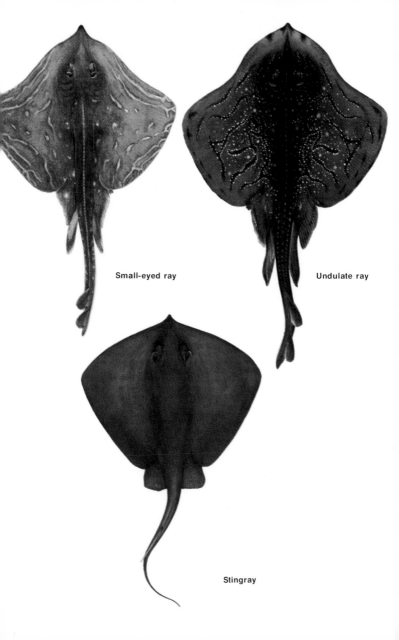

Small-eyed ray

Undulate ray

Stingray

The Sharks
Blue shark *Prionace glauca* (illustrated above)
Porbeagle shark *Lamna nasus*

Although five species of true shark make an appearance in our offshore waters, only two are regular visitors. The mako, thresher and hammerhead sharks will, no doubt, continue to make occasional visits but it is the blue shark and its portly near-relative the porbeagle that earn the interest of sea anglers. Each season, as the warm waters of the North Atlantic Drift exert their influence on the temperate zones, the blue shark arrives from the tropics. The species has a world-wide distribution. They grow to enormous weights farther south but the average rod-caught size around these islands seems to be around 60 lb (27 kg). From July to September this shark is the mainstay of tourist-orientated sharking. But it is unfortunate that the commercial charter operators provide their fishing guests with such heavy gear. It is not unusual to see the stiffest of boat rods coupled with big-game multiplying reels loaded with 130 lb (59 kg) braided lines. There can be no sport in using tackle of that strength.

The blue shark can fight well on light tackle, although there are many anglers who would put the tope ahead of this species in sporting terms. On a 30 lb (13.5 kg) class line rod and a reel capable of carrying at least 300 yd (274 m) of line, blue shark can be fought in a sporting manner. All sharks have sharp teeth and incredibly rough skins. Because of this we use long cable-laid wire traces between hook and reel line connection. I like to construct my traces from 150 lb (68 kg) breaking strain wire. A length of about 10 ft (3 m) is right from the hook link to the mid-trace swivel. Between the swivel and reel line I use long-liner's nylon of 250 lb (113 kg) b.s. to guard against the rough skin of the fish. You may feel that this trace material is far too heavy for a fish that weighs little more than the average wreck-caught conger eel. But the strength of the terminal rig is dictated by the mouth and skin of the shark rather than by the fighting ability of either species.

Shark fishing on the drift
Most blue shark fishing, and a lot of porbeagle angling, is done on the

(Right) *With a display of brute power, a porbeagle bends this angler's rod over the gunwhale in a tussle off the Isle of Wight where the species is known to haunt a deep trench in the area. This shark is more powerful than the blue and like all shark can be identified by its teeth.*

drift. The boat is allowed to drift along, driven by current sometimes but mostly by the wind, while a trail of mashed fish and oil called 'Rubby Dubby' is set up. This groundbaiting action spreads both smell and particles of oily food along a path behind the drifting boat. Sharks, swimming somewhere between midwater and the surface, detect the appetizing trail, then follow it up to find the source of food. The angler's bait, usually a whole mackerel, is suspended on a float. This can be a half inflated party balloon, or a purpose-made cork bung. The idea is that the bait can be set to a certain depth in the water. With more than one angler fishing, the baits would be suspended at different depths. The first a couple of fathoms below the surface, the second at twice that depth with the third much deeper in the water. We never know at what depth the shark are swimming, so it is sound practise to offer the baits at varied settings. Then, when a bite results we can alter the depth presentation to suit the arrival of the fish.

A bite is most often seen as a series of rapid jerks that my pull the float below the surface. Then the float will move away, across the water,

Trace for shark

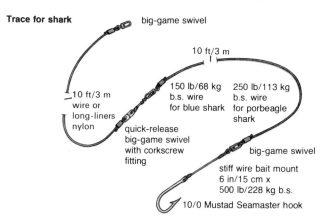

big-game swivel

10 ft/3 m

10 ft/3 m
wire or
long-liners
nylon

quick-release
big-game swivel
with corkscrew
fitting

150 lb/68 kg
b.s. wire
for blue shark

250 lb/113 kg
b.s. wire
for porbeagle
shark

big-game swivel

stiff wire bait mount
6 in/15 cm x
500 lb/228 kg b.s.

10/0 Mustad Seamaster hook

(Above left) *Groin pad and kidney harness—essential parts of the tackle for shark fishing.* (Left) *Stiff wire mounts can be fashioned using these twisted holding methods.* (Below) *Tie on the whole mackerel bait with strong thread at the tail wrist to prevent shark tearing it loose.*

before disappearing below the waves. This first run must be allowed to happen without pressure from the fisherman. His reel is out of gear with the ratchet set to give a sound signal that lets him follow the progress and judge the speed of the first run. As soon as the reel stops turning, the gear lever is engaged and the ratchet taken off. It it then wise to recover any slack line! As soon as the fish begins to move once more, the line tightens—and that is the time to strike hard. Obviously, the drag setting has been made before fishing commenced so that the second, powerful run will not smash the line. Let the fish make its second run against the pre-set drag. As it slows, add a little more drag by carefully adjusting the star drag setting. From now on it is a battle of give and take! When the fish is strong, let it take line from the reel under controlled drag pressure. As it weakens and begins to turn, the angler must fight back.

Porbeagle shark

Both the blue and porbeagle shark can put up a good fight that tests the skill and strength of the angler. If the hooked fish is a big fellow the fight will be easier handled if the angler is wearing a groin pad and kidney harness to protect the body against the bruising effect of a protracted struggle.

Trolling techniques

The porbeagle shark is generally larger and more widespread in our seas. It can be looked on as a cold water species, for this fish is found as far north as Norway and seems to be around all year. Fish of 500 lb (227 kg) have been caught in British waters, so the porbeagle is truly a big-game shark. The fishing method is similar to that used for blue shark, with the possible exception of some sharking done off the west coast of Ireland. There, trolling a bait just below the surface has proved a taking method. The shark grounds have a number of underwater reefs that seem to be the favoured habitat of these large porbeagles. Trolled baits are slowly moved over the peaks of the reef. The resident porgies, feeding on the pollack, see the baits travelling through the surface film, rise up in the water and hit them hard! While I was fishing this way, I had a number of flexible wire traces bitten through. I think this happened as the fish tore in and grabbed the hookbait. Unlike the drifted bait, which the shark has time to inspect, a trolled bait is taken in one gulp. If the wire happens to lie across those murderous teeth, there is little chance of it surviving the first bite. I've now adapted the traces to have a stiff wire 'teething piece', 6 in (152 mm) long, between hook and flexible wire trace.

The most dangerous time when shark fishing is that moment when the fish has to be subdued and brought aboard the boat. As most shark fishing is done from seagoing charter boats the skipper has the task of boating the fish, for it is a job for an expert. Many sharks are gaffed, which kills them, but there is a move to using a tailing rope to slip around the body of the fish. Once in place, the fish can be hauled inboard and the hook removed. The specimen can then be returned to the sea.

Common skate *Raja batis*

At one time fishing for those huge skate that were common to the west of Ireland and the Northern Isles, was rated as the measure of an angler's ability to cope with big fish. Unfortunately, what we anglers didn't realize was that these fish are relatively thin on the ground. Years of rod and line fishing effectively reduced the numbers of skate at the well-known marks. The Inland Fisheries Trust, who control the Irish Record List, removed the species from among those fish that qualified for specimen awards. This went a long way to reducing the angling pressure on the big skate. In Britain, it was suggested to anglers and commercial fishermen by the angling journals and charter skippers that the species was in danger and deserved being returned to the sea if caught. There is a sign that the huge specimens *are* coming back, so there may well be skate fishing, of quality, in future years. This is one fish that can truly test the angler. The fish isn't fast and furious . . . it's more a ponderous muscle-tearing fight that may have you praying for divine help!

Skate are bottom-feeders that rarely leave the sanctuary of broken ground. The species feeds by flopping their immense bulk down over their prey, to smother the food while they jockey their bodies into position. The mouth of all skates is far back from the point of the snout. The distance involves the fish in measuring just how far back the body has to be wriggled in order to get the food within their mouths. This behaviour can be of help to the skate fisherman. If he is paying attention to his rod tip, the skate angler will see it dip sharply as the fish noses up to the hookbait and then falls onto it. As the skate adjusts its position to swallow the bait, the rod tip will indicate this by a series of dipping motions. Time has to be allowed before a strike is made because this species is notoriously slow in mouthing the bait. After all, no live fish would escape from a skate after it had crushed down onto the seabed! As soon as there is any movement suggesting that the skate is moving off, I strike. The problem is to then lift the fish at least 3 ft (1 m) from the seabed to get some water under its body. Achieving that will prevent the fish from 'gluing' itself to the ground. A large specimen will make repeated efforts to get back to the seabed. These strong runs must be held on the drag of the reel. To tire a skate, the fish must be allowed to move but *not* to get into a position of stalemate. As a skate begins to lose its strength the fish stops swimming horizontally. It then hangs in the water. The line-hook angle changes, because the skate's mouth is about a quarter of the way back from its snout. This change in fighting angle is made worse as the current presses against the fish's huge body. When this happens, many skate fishers maintain drag pressure to cause the fish to 'kite' up in the tide.

A beaten fish will rise to the surface well downtide from the boat. There it gets a rest unless further pumping pressure is brought to bear. Dragging a hundredweight (50 kg) of skate across the top of the water puts a fantastic strain on man and gear. The only alternative is for the boat to drop back to the fish as the angler progressively recovers line. With conservation in mind gaffing must be a careful procedure. Ideally, two fellow anglers should gaff the fish neatly by securely pinning each wing. The fish can be lifted into the boat with the minimum of fuss. No harm will result, but keep the gaffs away from the body cavity which contains the fish's vital organs. There is evidence that skate caught and released come to no harm and do not migrate far from their chosen habitat. This accounts for them being easily over-fished but if we return the giants there will be skate living and breeding in numbers, ensuring a future for the species.

The moment when great care must be taken, for large common skate are powerful fish. Here, the gaff is being applied to a common skate caught in a tide race off Kinsale Old Head, southern Ireland.

Smooth hounds
Common *Mustelus mustelus* (illustrated above)
Starry *Mustelus asterias*

In recent years we have identified two separate species of smooth hounds that visit our shores as summer comes to the shallow, inshore waters. Although wide in their distribution over the North Atlantic, these fish appear to favour only a few locations. The estuaries of the Blackwater, Crouch and Thames all receive shoals of these skate-toothed dogfish. The two species live almost entirely on crustaceans, for which their crushing jaws are perfectly designed. Crabs, prawns, lobsters and shellfish of many species figure in the fishes' diet.

I treat them as I would the lesser-spotted dogfish, though they have the strength and power of the bull huss. The fish puts up a dour, extended struggle using the tidal flow and their over-size fins to beat the rod. A fish of 28 lb (12.5 kg) was landed from the Thames Estuary in 1980 and a commercial netsman returned a smooth hound of over 30 lb (13.5 kg) that he caught on the Outer Sands. It is possible that this dogfish is more numerous than we think. Perhaps our traditional fish and worm baits are rejected and in the flat, sandy areas, a concentration with crab hookbaits could produce more smooth hounds for the rod and line fisherman.

Terminal rigs can be of heavy gauge nylon, constructed as a running leger because smooth hounds hug the bottom closely. I have an idea that this species of dogfish does not like waterborne noise or mud-clouded water for it is not often taken in trawl nets and the uptide casters seem to catch more of them than do other sea anglers.

The distinctive jaw and tooth pattern of the smooth hound. In common with other dogfish it is a bottom feeder but prefers crustaceans and worms rather than fish.

Spurdog or Piked dogfish *Squalus acanthias*

A live-bearing member of the lesser sharks, this fish is usually hated by
sea anglers. Roaming the oceans in vast shoals, the spurdog is a vicious
predator with an enormous shoal appetite. These fish can easily denude
a sea area of all but the largest fish. Distributed throughout the North
Atlantic, the fish arrive in shallow coastal waters in late spring. Luckily
for anglers, the commercial fishermen of many countries wreak a terrible
harvest on the species as the flesh is sweet and there are no bones. Care
has to be taken when handling the spurdog. In front of each dorsal fin
there is a sharp spur which can cause a nasty wound that may well fester
as the spur is said to have venomous properties. Identification is simple
when we see the fish's spurs but it also differs from the other dogfish in
that it lacks an anal fin.

Nobody really seeks to fish for the species, for in truth they find the
angler. When they arrive, there is little point in not fishing for them as
they are capable of putting on a fair struggle when the tackle is light.
They swim between the surface and the bottom, wherever they find
food. I used to fish with a wire trace, trying to avoid the cutting action of
the fish's teeth but after many frustrating sessions I found that the fish
tangled the terminal rig into a hopeless mess. Their movements are so
vigorous as to kink any wire, no matter how pliable. I now use a double-
hook rig formed in strong nylon. Two droppers lead from a three-way
swivel and are tied in 50 lb (22.5 kg) nylon.

After catching a few fish, you will find that the nylon is so badly frayed
as to need constant replacement. Line is cheap, so pay attention to the
condition of the terminal rig throughout your fishing. The rod/reel
combination can be a 20 lb (9 kg) outfit. It will cope handsomely with the
spurdog, letting them make short, jerking runs from the boat. The two
baited hooks aren't there to catch two fish at a time. The problem is that
spurdog are adept at tearing any bait from a hook without getting
themselves attached. Two hookbaits allow one to be lost but are ready
for the fish when it makes its next attack.

Unhooking the fish is a time for care. It is best achieved by holding the

Double-hook rig for spurdog

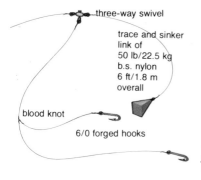

three-way swivel

trace and sinker
link of
50 lb/22.5 kg
b.s. nylon
6 ft/1.8 m
overall

blood knot

6/0 forged hooks

(Above) *The 'Valley' disgorger
can be useful in getting hooks
from spurdog and other species.*
(Left) *Spurdog paternoster rig.*

spurdog flat on the deck while the trace is kept taut. Never let the fish
twist and thrash around at the end of a line, for those spurs will
inevitably be driven into somebody's arm. Get a strong disgorger and
remove the hook cleanly and quickly. Some anglers have a nasty habit of
snipping off the fish's spurs with pliers before returning the fish over the
side. Don't do this, for the fish will be denied its defence mechanism.
Bait is no problem for this species, they will take anything that is offered.
Being a predator, all fishbait will be grabbed eagerly but they happily
mop up worm and crustacean hookbaits.

Tope *Galeorhinus galeus*

The tope is our most sporting representative of the lesser shark group of
fishes. Among sea anglers it enjoys a reputation as the speedy one, a
fighter that makes long, reel-stripping runs to tax the skill and tackle of
many an angler. Tope are found practically everywhere in the world.
I've caught them in places as far apart as Gibraltar and Norway and I'm
told that the same species is present in the Far East. The fish can be
identified by its sleek body shape and deeply notched lower tail lobe.
Fresh from the water, the tope is a steely-grey but this colour soon fades
to a dirty hue after the fish dies. Tope are live bearers. They breed by

internal fertilization, the female fish carrying 40 or more pups which she releases in shallow water during the warm summer months. I once undertook a tagging exercise, catching baby tope on a spinning rod in the shallow channels off the Essex coast. In all, I tagged over 50 of these streamlined babies but, alas, I've yet to have a single tag returned to me. Each little fish weighed about 5 lb (2 kg), measuring 2 ft (60 cm) from head to tail.

This fish is a predator upon bottom-dwelling fodder fish. Understandably, we copy this behaviour by applying leger principles to the rig. One can use a wire or high breaking-strain nylon trace. Personally, I choose nylon, tying up the hook trace to 80 lb (36 kg) monofilament which withstands the stresses placed on the trace during the struggle.

Trace for tope

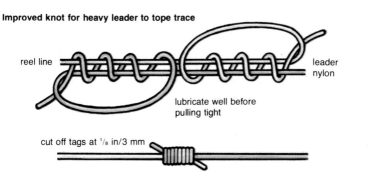

Improved knot for heavy leader to tope trace

(Top) *Tope traces can be constructed from cable-laid wire or quality nylon. When casting from shore, increase the hook trace to 5 ft (1.5 m) and dispense with the second trace length.*
(Above) *Shore fishing for tope can be very successful using a heavy trace and leader, 14 ft (4 m) of 80 lb (36 kg) b.s. nylon tied in this improved knot.*

Tope fishing from the shore

Around the European coastline there are a lot of places, where tope will come right onto the tideline. Usually they are following shoal fish but I know of situations where tope enter estuaries to feed on flounders. They are not known to tolerate freshwater, though it seems that it doesn't bother them. Tope do not advertise their presence in these shallow waters. I first knew they were to be found in an Essex rivermouth when a hooked flattie was ripped from the hook. A change in terminal rig, together with the sacrifice of an earlier caught flounder as a bait, brought me to a tope of nearly 30 lb (13.5 kg). Sandy beaches, with a prolific bait and fish population, might well be the first place to seek this species. Rock marks, where the hard shoreline juts out onto clean ground, is another environment where this fish will patrol the seabed to seek out species that live there.

I use my cod beachcaster on serious shore toping expeditions. The length, 12 ft (3.5 m), gives control of the tope with that extra absorbtion of the fighting tactics that this fish can display. One expects long, stripping runs from them, for they cannot escape the line pressure by diving – there is nowhere to dive to in shallow water. Expect fast movement at distance and have enough nylon on the multiplier to cope with it. I use a reel that has a capacity of 350 yd (320 m) of 18 lb (8 kg). To this, I add a lengthy casting leader (that also acts as the terminal trace), of 50 lb (22.5 kg) nylon. A link barrel swivel is inserted 4 ft (120 cm) from the hook so that a landed fish can be quickly detached from the rig. Getting the hook out of a lively tope can be a hassle, especially if the fish is still attached to the reel line and rod! A quick-release trace makes the task a good deal easier to accomplish. I have illustrated the system with a wire trace as there are many anglers who use this form of end rig.

(Left) *Conceal the bulk of the hook inside the body of the bait. Use elasticated thread to tie the bait to the terminal trace. It will not deter the fish.*
(Right) *When tope fishing from the shore, wire traces can be joined to the leader using this special kind of split link swivel. Its advantage is that in emergency it can be released quickly.*

A beach rodrest is invaluable when tope fishing. I cast the lash of fishbait as far as I can, then set the rod almost perpendicular in the rest. This will show any small nodding on the tip that indicates the arrival of a feeding tope, while keeping the line clear of inshore wave action that also creates a rod-tip movement. The reel is taken out of gear, with the ratchet set on. If a fish takes the bait, the first indication is at the rod tip, then the ratchet will buzz as the fish begins to move away. There is time to pick the rod up while flicking the ratchet off. This is important, as fish may feel a vibration running down the line. Some reels have an extremely coarse ratchet that requires a strong pull to get the spool turning. Control of the line peeling off the spool is done by lightly thumbing the drum as it turns.

Timing the strike is important. Hit the gear-engaging lever as soon as the first run stops. If the line is taut, strike hard over the shoulder; a small amount of slack can be taken up by moving smartly back up the beach. The second run will be faster and probably longer as the tope feels your hook. The fight progresses as a series of runs that gradually diminish in length as the fish tires. When you feel this happening, apply a little more drag while recovering line back on to the drum. Don't be too hasty to see the fish, remembering that tope are tough and can produce the final, desperate movement that has caught many an angler completely unaware. A steady pumping action with sensitive drag control will bring your fish into the beach. When it finally arrives keep a reasonably tight line under thumb pressure. Ask a fishing companion to move round behind the fish where he can grasp the tail wrist and lift it clear of the water. Gaffs are neither necessary nor humane, so recover the hook and release the tope to provide sport elsewhere. The tope is not a food species, so put them back.

Quick-release split-link swivel

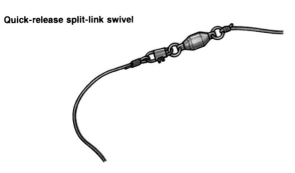

Tope angling from a boat

Although a powerful adversary, the tope does not give the best fight from a boat unless the angler is fishing over shallow ground or using light tackle methods. A 20 lb (9 kg) class rod/reel combination will handle all but the largest fish. You will find this sporting gear unpopular when from a crowded boat other anglers have to reel in their tackle to give you time and clear water in which to fight the fish. Patience on their part is vital, as a hooked tope can rush around under the boat making a terrible mess of other lines.

The fishing technique is the same as one would use from the shore. Strike when the first run fades. A delay, or deliberate wait for the start of a second run, can end in a gut-hooked fish, something that nobody wants! I believe that timing on the strike is the most important aspect of tope fishing, closely followed by handling of the fight when the fish is almost at the side of the boat. It is then that the unwary angler can be caught out, either by having a clutch that is screwed down too tight or by letting the tope thrash and twist off the hook because of inexperience when boating the specimen. Take a firm grip on the tail and dorsal, swinging the fish over the gunwhale onto the deck.

(Left) *Tope fishing is an exciting sport, for the fish will continue to fight after being boated.* (Below) *A tope being returned to the water by Jim McLanaghan, fishing off the Mull of Galloway. The species should always be put back.*

Turbot   Brill

Turbot *Psetta maximus*
Brill *Scophthalmus rhombus*

The turbot is a fish of the offshore sandbanks that lie in deep water. It has a wide distribution, being found off the coast of Western Europe as far north as Holland. This highly prized flatfish grows to over 50 lb (22.5 kg), second only to the halibut as the largest flattie. It is a slow-moving fish that lies half-buried in the sands to avoid the swift currents that sweep the banks. From there it ambushes the luckless sandeels and other small fish that are caught up in the tide. It is easily identified as a left-handed species, meaning that the eyes and dark coloration are on the fish's left side and the mouth opens to the left when the body and head are facing away from you. Only the brill is similar in body shape but it has a smooth skin, whereas the turbot is covered in bony tubercles.

Fishing for turbot can be an exacting task. Positioning of the fishing craft, relative to a known turbot mark, is critical. The fish lie on the downtide side of the bank to avoid the maximum pressure exerted by the tidal flow. Anglers try to anchor on or in front of the top of the bank. From here they let a legered bait, usually a fillet of fresh mackerel, trundle back downtide to a position over the lip of the highest sand. Their object is to simulate the arrival of a small fish. Waiting turbot

Correct boat position over sandbank

tide

small fish are swept
over the peaks

move forward, shoot out their cavernous mouths to engulf the bait. The bite is often felt as a sudden dipping pressure on the rod tip. A pause to let the fish get a firm grip and the strike is made.

Turbot cannot be said to be plucky fighters. They are heavy in the water, lying across the run of tide and placing a heavy strain on the tackle and angler's muscles. Steady pumping pressure will bring the fish up through the water where they will often kite up to the surface many yards behind the boat. Because of this likelihood I tend to choose a 30 lb (13.5 kg) rod combination to give me a little in hand. Power is needed to beat the environment rather than the fish! A leger rig is necessary, with one or two hooks of about 6/0 or larger. The turbot has a large mouth and will accept a whole mackerel lash readily. Form the terminal rig in nylon (see dab), 30 lb (13.5 kg) monofilament with hooks at 4 ft (1 m) apart. Turbot specialists will tell you that this fish always lies in groups and the possibility is that you can hook more than a single fish. I have done that on two occasions but I doubt whether the chance will come in the future as this species is sought after by the professional fisherman to the extent that most of our famous marks, such as the Shambles Bank at Portland, are fished out.

The sandbanks can be a dangerous place for the novice boatman. Take great care before lowering the anchor. Avoid the boil where the racing water shoots to the surface as it forces its way over the bank. Your boat's position should be well uptide anyway as the boil is naturally swept downtide of the actual high spot of the bank. An echo sounder is invaluable to provide a profile of the underwater topography. The hardest part of any turbot or brill fishing is locating the right place to position the boat relative to the fish and tide.

(Left) *This jubilant French angler has caught a turbot from a Youghal mark, off the coast of Co. Cork.* (Below) *A correctly positioned boat allows angling over fish feeding on the sandbank.*

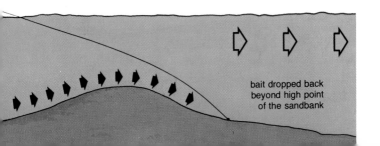

bait dropped back
beyond high point
of the sandbank

Whiting *Merlangius merlangus*

Whiting are a common fish in the North Atlantic area. They frequent soft and sandy seabeds in huge, voracious shoals where they harry the clouds of minute fry that form the bulk of the species' diet. Whiting are more inclined to take fish than other members of the cod family. The species arrives off the British Isles in the late autumn to feed in depths of 10–20 fathoms (18–36 m). Whiting can be found throughout the year, where the sea is of greater depth. They are recognized by their sleek body, silvery flanks and brownish back. Whiting have no barbule. The teeth are incredibly sharp and small, which aids them when tearing angler's baits to shreds while tangling terminal rigs into a mess that can defy description.

Small strips of fishbait, herring, mackerel and sprat, are perfect baits on small hooks. The fish will take marine worms, particularly when close inshore where they forage into depths of only a couple of fathoms. Use paternoster tackle (see cod) when fishing slackish tides from a boat. This species swims slightly higher in the water than the ground-feeding cod and haddock, where they find the fry of their own and many other fishes. Whiting are an important part of the catch of anglers and trawlermen. Arriving inshore before the cod, they bulk up catches but do not have any serious reputation as a fighter on the average tackle used by the shore or boat fisherman. Contrary to opinion, this fish can be a tasty meal if cooked within a few hours of capture.

Whiting can be taken on small pirks with or without baited hooks. They are also known to start feeding when the tide is slack, so anglers waiting for the action when the tide begins to move sometimes get a pleasant surprise. A good mark for this unfashionable species is Llandwyn beach, Anglesey, North Wales.

Ballan wrasse *Labrus bergylta*

The ballan wrasse has gained steadily in reputation among shore fisherman for a decade or more. Even though considered by many as inedible, this species has established itself as a fighter within its chosen environment. It is a fish of the foulest ground. The rocky coasts of Europe, especially those that are southerly or west-facing, provide the fish with an ideal habitat while giving the angler a fishing situation that has both danger and challenge. Under the towering cliffs of the west we find an inshore seabed littered with the fallen debris of milleniums. Among the tangle of marine growth and boulders the wrasse makes its home and it is from this graveyard of tackle that we attempt to catch the brilliantly-coloured fish.

Ballan wrasse are the largest of a group of fish within the genus. They vary tremendously in colour, much of the variation being environmental. There have been green, brown and red specimens, which has caused many people to describe them as different species. Thick-bodied, with hard, huge scales the ballan wrasse has a long dorsal fin, spiky in the front and soft-rayed toward the fish's tail. One of the interesting anatomical features of the wrasse is its mouth. The upper and lower jaws carry a row of powerful, tearing teeth that it uses to remove limpets and other gastropods from the rocks. There are further crushing teeth in the gullet, which aid the wrasse in reducing the shellfish to a digestible state.

Wrasse are unusual fish in that they construct a nest at breeding times. Large eggs, over 1 mm in diameter, are deposited within the nest made of seaweed that has been joined with mucus then jammed into any crevice that the fish can find. From May to October the species lives in shallow water. Being very territorial in behaviour, they stay close to

(Above) *A perfect wrasse habitat at Green Island, on the Clare coast. Deep water lies right below the angler's feet, under the flat shelves of rock.*
(Left) *Ballan wrasse display a range of superb colours, their body chemistry responding to the habitat in which they live.*
(Right) *A simple running leger rig for fishing clean, unobstructed seabed. When possible always attempt to keep terminal tackles as simple as possible. They save time tackling up.*

their chosen feeding and breeding site. There are two basic wrasse fishing techniques; float fishing or placing a hookbait onto the seabed. Both methods have their adherents but I must admit to preferring a suspended bait approach. There is something fascinating about watching a float that is pulled and swept in the path of the wild waves. For me, timing the strike reaction to a bite is easier than gauging when to hit a soft tap to the rod tip!

Float fishing for ballan wrasse

I choose my 10 ft (3 m) carp/pike rod because it has the strength to strike over distance, and the power to apply pressure against a wrasse that bores deep to escape the tethering effect on its mouth. A fixed-spool reel suits me, but a multiplying reel will handle the casting necessary for there is weight in both the float and the sinker that takes the bait down. It is vital to use a sea float that has sufficient buoyancy to ride the waves without pulling under as the crest of each swell punches past it. Long casting may be called for, so I have adapted the terminal rig to use two separate barrel swivels. The idea was given to me by a Channel Isles angler from Guernsey, where they do a lot of rock angling, who guaranteed that it gives far fewer tangles as the rig flies through the air.

To stop the wisp of nylon, left when tying the knot, from catching within the hollow tube of the float I have added a bead. The depth setting for the bait is adjusted by tying-in a stop knot or piece of rubber band to the reel line. A stop knot is best when the depth setting has to be constantly re-adjusted to suit tide and long-cast over a varied ground.

Rig for wrasse

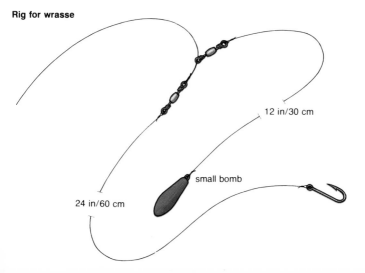

12 in/30 cm

small bomb

24 in/60 cm

Accurate depth finding to within a few inches or centimetres is not necessary or, at times, possible. But don't worry, because the wrasse will soon rise in the water when they see a mouthful above their heads. In fact, there will be a lot of fish swimming along the face of underwater ledges searching for molluscs to tear off. Wrasse are not hook shy. They will grab a bait and take the float down hard, so the business of avoiding friction on the float at the time of striking is not as important as it might be with the sea's delicate feeders.

Hooking fish can be said to be easy, but keeping the wrasse out of the maze of rocks and weed isn't! I play them hard for the first minute to lift their heads and when this has been achieved give them a lot less rod pressure: then the wrasse will show its merit, making boring runs to get back to the seabed that it knows so well. Take your landing net along on a wrasse expedition. You cannot lift a deadweight on the float rod and it is ridiculous to apply a long-handled gaff to these sea carp! After inspecting the ballan, let it go immediately.

There are, of course, times when a distance-casting rig becomes more efficient. Make up a nylon link-leger rig that has a 'rotten bottom' connection between sliding barrel swivel and sinker. Then, if the lead gets caught up, it is fairly easy to break out without losing the rest of the terminal tackle. A slim leger weight will be less prone to jamming up in foul ground than the conical or pyramid-shaped leads. I always hold my rod when wrasse fishing. It helps to prevent the waves having too marked an effect on the rod tip and controls my choice of time to strike. With the rod in the hands, detecting the arrival of the fish, its first mouthing of the bait and the moment when it has taken it, all become more positive. Fewer fish are able to take the gear into a hole or kelp bed—which causes less frustration to you, the angler!

Wrasse are fish that have no defined feeding time. I've caught them far into the dark hours when I thought only pollack were about. It must be an instinct among those fish that live on rocky ground to search for food at night. The conger eel is the other exponent of killing its neighbour after dark. Anyway, if you do fish at night, watch where you place your feet. Inspect the terrain before the light fades so that you know exactly where the gullies and slippery ledges are. Although wrasse are shellfish feeders, I find that most of my fishing for them is done with worm, soft crab and cocktail baits. Limpets are one of the fish's natural diets but I only use them to lock a worm or other soft bait onto the hook. It is probable that wrasse feed mostly by sight, by scraping shells off the rocks. The angler's bait is smell-attractive, which pulls fish toward it, and is why some oily groundbait can produce fantastic catches.

(Above) *Sunset over Derrynane Harbour, Co Kerry, scene of some of Ireland's best wrasse angling.* (Right) *A wrasse fishing float rig for the foul ground. The large drilled bullet head is trapped between two barrel swivels that prevent the weight tangling during the cast.* (Below) *rock fishing puts considerable strain on the knots used in many terminal rigs. Knots are the weakest link in the chain. This is a simple hitch that resists the loose, slipping tendency of many far more complicated knots.*

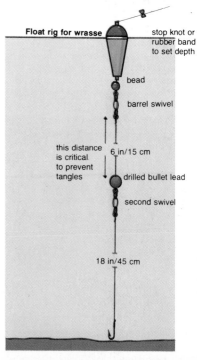

Float rig for wrasse

stop knot or rubber band to set depth

bead

barrel swivel

this distance is critical to prevent tangles

6 in/15 cm

drilled bullet lead

second swivel

18 in/45 cm

Hitch knot

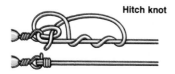

SEA ANGLING COMPETITIONS

Throughout time sea fishing has been a competitive sport, with man against fish producing the keenest of contests. During the last decade, there has been a move toward extending the skills of the sport by the introduction of timed competitions. Inevitably this has led to international competitive events such as the European Championships, where teams of sea anglers from many countries—some travelling from behind the Iron Curtain—match their wits against the fish and the elements. In 1981, the championships were held at Scheveningen, in Holland, where boat anglers fished the lower North Sea for cod and whiting.

Shorefishing has shown the greatest advances in match angling. Again, the international element is strong, with anglers competing from countries that do not possess any seaboard at all. Many nationalities fish the Tylers International which is held, annually, at different venues around the Irish coast. Each spring, match anglers travel to Folkestone, on the south coast of England for the popular European and All England Sea Angling event. As many as 1,000 shorecasters spread themselves over 7 miles (11 km) of Kent's shingle beaches. Apart

from the heightened atmosphere that is created by the different languages, many tackle ideas and fishing methods are exchanged between the sportsmen. As they fish they discuss the merits of systems created to cope with the vagaries of species and water conditions that are found on both sides of the English Channel.

Travelling abroad to fish can be an expensive business. But with an increased national interest many countries and individual companies are providing an element of sponsorship to get their anglers to overseas contests. The controlling bodies of the sport, like the National Federation of Sea Anglers in England, select their representative teams on the basis of the record of each angler in local and nationwide fishing matches. Angling is thought not to be a spectator sport but there is evidence that television and other media now realize that there are more adherents to angling than any other form of outdoor sport. The coverage of angling should ensure a greater international following for the future.

(Below left) *Competitors in the European and All England Sea Angling Championships fill the shingle beaches from Folkestone to Dymchurch, in Kent.* (Below) *Craft leaving Cobh, Ireland, with competitors in a deepsea match.*

(Above) *Small and large boats of all shapes and kinds are put into service as angling craft. Some are suitable and designed for the job, but many are not.* (Below) *A sea-angling dinghy must be a stable fishing platform when it is at anchor and while drift-fishing, but also capable of getting its occupants home safely when the weather turns bad and the seas become rough.*

THE SEA ANGLER'S DINGHY

Although many anglers use the services of a charter boat and skipper on their deepsea adventures, there is an ever-growing army of sportsmen who go to sea in their own small craft. Fishing dinghies fall into two categories: displacement hulls that sit in the water, and planing boats that have the ability to ride on the surface with very little of the hull immersed when under power. Each type of craft has its advantages. In a choppy sea the traditional displacement dinghy is very stable, but it cannot go faster through the water than its theoretical hull speed, no matter how many horsepower is contained within the outboard engine.

The planing hull, as typified by the high-speed runabouts, achieves high speed by planing on the surface; but at rest, when most of our fishing is done, the boat does not enjoy the same stability as the dinghy. Fortunately, there are hybrid semi-planing hulls that have the best characteristics of both forms of dinghy.

At one time, all fishing dinghies were made of wood, clinker built from planks laid overlapping each other on a strong frame. They demand care in use and annual maintenance such as scraping and painting. Fibreglass dinghies require a lot less looking after. A new material has appeared on the angling scene—aluminium. For years the Americans have used aluminum boats of all kinds. The craft are immensely strong, need no maintenance beyond periodic cleaning and produce a great fuel saving. That factor alone makes them a serious contender for the fishing dinghy purchaser. Having less weight than the other hull materials, the aluminium boat is easier to push through the water. Less power requirement means a smaller outboard engine using far less costly fuel. One other advantage is that a 16 ft (5 m) sea angling boat can be transported on the top of a car.

Commonsense and a clear knowledge of what the boat is expected to do will dictate the size of dinghy suitable for sea fishing. I operate on the premise that the weight of fishing gear carried adds up to at least another man. I like to see a lot of space in a dinghy, space into which the occupants can move when necessary. This is vitally important. Mobility in the boat ensures that the anchor man or the chap on the engine can react and move swiftly to counteract a problem. The crowded dinghies so often seen at holidays and weekends leave no allowance for the unforeseen happening. We haven't, as yet, applied legislation to set out the number of anglers to a boat. There are recommendations but they are often ignored. For me, a 16 ft (5 m) dinghy is made for two anglers, their tackle, a possible catch of fish and a large allowance for safety.

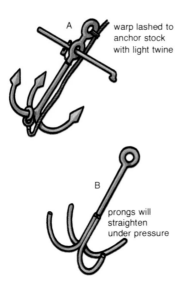

A warp lashed to anchor stock with light twine

B prongs will straighten under pressure

C 6 ft/1.8 m of chain

(Above and left) *Anchoring. The Fisherman (A) for broken ground. The trip enables it to be pulled out backwards if it fouls. The mild steel grapnel (B) for rocky bottoms. The anchor (C) is right for sand and mud but needs 6ft (1.8m) of chain to lay the anchor flat on the bottom.*

No matter how much buoyancy the boat has, or how experienced the owner, *lifejackets for the anglers are a must*. The sudden movement of the sea rarely upsets the boat, but it does often throw the occupants out! The type of life-jacket worn depends on the particular watersport. Anglers need to keep their arms unhampered so the inflatable unit is desirable. A halter jacket combined with a CO_2 inflation system does not restrict movement very much. Recent advances in the protective clothing industry have given us flotation suits, where the one-piece garment ensures survival in the worst possible weather, while ensuring the wearer stays afloat. There is a degree of fashion built into these suits, too. Gone is the inflated 'Teddy Bear' appearance!

(Left) *The 'Thermotic' suit provides foul-weather protection and is a superb buoyancy aid.* (Above) *The aluminium dinghy is seaworthy, fast and needs little maintenance.* (Below) *After each outing, flush outboard engines through by running them in freshwater for at least five minutes to remove the salt from the cooling system.*

(Right) *The blinking neon echo sounder will provide an enormous amount of information about the kind of seabed over which the boat is moving, as well as the depth of water below the boat. Here, the signal indicates a rocky bottom with fish showing at two depths.*
(Below) *Three methods of fixing a transducer. Two of them are permanent fixtures to the hull, the other is a removable bracket which hinges over the bows.*

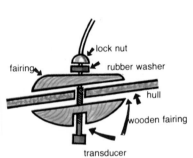

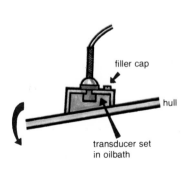

Fixing a transducer

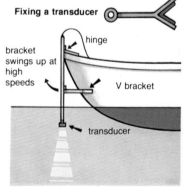

FISH FINDING

For years finding a known fishing mark was a question of establishing cross-reference points on the shoreline. Two easily seen buildings, or similar visible marks, were lined up to give one line of sight. Then another line was established to bring the boat to a chosen position. At best the system was accurate to a few hundred yards (200 m) or so when inshore. At distances over five miles (8 km), the mark sailed to could be half a mile (800 m) out. Dead reckoning and the boat's yawing across the tide added to what was in effect a hit-and-miss affair.

Then along came electronic aids. Decca Navigator units began to appear in the wheelhouses of charter boats but were far too expensive for the small-boat owner. The echo sounder was the answer to his navigational problem. In association with bearings taken from the shore, the sounder gave the opportunity to traverse the seabed until suitable readings on the chart, or blips on the dial, indicated the correct depth. What early sounders could not do was to show fish or a clear-cut trace of the seabed, and most of these units lacked power. Modern echo sounders are infinitely better at showing what lies below the keel. Micro-electronics, with improved circuits, give us instruments that greatly aid our understanding of the seabed while showing shoals if not individual fish. Obviously, the echo sounder is no replacement for boating skills, but used intelligently it can play a useful role in improving catches.

The flasher impulse unit needs understanding. An impulse is transmitted down to the sea bed. It hits the mud or rock bottom, is reflected back to a gathering device on the hull and then the time taken for the return journey of the signal is electronically converted to become a flashing blip on a graduated scale. These sounders are ideal as indicators of depth but, until recently, did not have enough power to give a clear-cut signal with separation of targets. With higher power output and a much shorter pulse length, the modern sounder can show shoals and even individual fish, and that is what the angler needs. With experience, fishermen can read the blips appearing on the sounder scale as signals returning from a variety of types of seabed. They isolate fish in midwater, detect weed growth and recognize underwater shapes more easily. So the sounder becomes more than just an aid to depth finding and fishing mark recognition.

Given the choice most anglers would choose a graph sounder, one that builds a picture on paper of the seabed. They are more expensive to purchase and have an ongoing operation cost in terms of graph paper

Cobh Harbour can be fished when the seas outside are rough and unfishable. Here a thornback is being drawn to the waiting net.

rolls. What they do is to present a gradually emerging, permanent record of what lies on the sea floor together with fish shoals above it. The graph is easy to read, makes the recognition of wreck and reef more positive. Subsequent visits to the mark can be more easily made as an earlier graphic record can be used as the comparison chart builds up.

One problem experienced by the newcomer to graph sounders is that the picture of the seabed differs when the speed of the boat over the ground varies. After finding an underwater obstruction, careful inspection can be made by adopting a constant, fine searching speed that produces greater resolution and separation on the paper trace, or flashing screen, of the various parts of a wreck or reef. Sounders are by no means the complete answer to pinpointing angling marks. Nothing can replace experience and local knowledge but, in association with established land bearings, they can vastly improve the fish-catching ability of any angler. Incidentally, I get a great deal of satisfaction from coming to know—with accuracy—the conformation of my local seabed. You would be surprised at the number of unexplained obstructions that litter the fishing grounds.

SAFETY

I never cease to be astonished at the antics of some sea anglers, whether fishing from boats or casting their baits from the shoreline. At times there appears to be a total disregard for the basic rules of commonsense and their own personal safety. Why some people insist on wearing thigh boots in a dinghy or on the deck of a low-gunwaled fishing vessel defeats logic. When filled with water, these *shore angling* waders rapidly become two anchors that can rapidly take anybody below the surface. Easily slipped-off rubber boots or calf length ones are most suitable protection for the feet.

There are anglers who carry a lifejacket to sea but never wear it on the basis that it hampers movement. They say that no boat sinks immediately and that they would have time to put the thing on. That is probably true of an incident involving a large vessel or motorized fishing vessel (MFV). Accidents to dinghies are never sinkings. They are the sudden swell that swamps a small boat or the submerged rock that *throws the unwary occupant out* of the craft. It is a clever man who can find his lifejacket and put it on when he is trying to keep his head above water! You only have one life and need buy only one jacket, so wear it.

A number of shoreline anglers are lost every year by being cut-off by the tide. The answer is to watch the progress of the flood tide while knowing exactly where the escape route lies. Similarly, the rock fisher must not fish on until the sea is driving up a sheer cliff face. Learn where the safe climbs are, remembering that a hurried scamper up the cliffs is difficult when the gear and a possible catch has to be carried. The sea is intolerant of fools. Come to know its power and understand its moods: it then becomes a source of sporting pleasure to the thinking angler.

The nasty lesser weever has venomous dorsal spines that cause very painful wounds. A visit to the doctor is usually necessary.

THE TRAVELLING SEA ANGLER

It is a fact that sea anglers travel greater distances, on a regular basis, to find their fishing than either coarse or game anglers. It is also true to say that much of Europe's quality sea angling takes place around the islands of the North Atlantic. The mainland of Britain, Ireland, Isles of Shetland and Orkney and the Channel Islands together with the more northerly waters of Iceland and Greenland can produce fishing that is unrivalled on the Continental seaboard.

Fishing is now an important area of tourism. Holidaymakers and established anglers are prone to add their mass of tackle to the already over-loaded family suitcases. This necessity to carry adequate fishing gear determines how we travel to the other islands to satisfy our sporting desires. Airlines set an unrealistic weight limit on the travelling sportsman, so most of us elect to journey by sea. With a car our travels can be readily undertaken on one of the numerous car ferries that operate from Britain.

Anglers looking to the south and west of Ireland—which has been called an angler's paradise—are well served by overnight ferries. The journey by car is relatively quick as Ireland can be crossed in just a few hours. Some of the most interesting sea fishing is from the off-shore isles. Achill Island and Valencia are joined to the mainland by bridges, Dursey by a cable car and the smaller Aran Islands can be reached by boat and light aircraft.

Vast stretches of unexplored fishing beaches and many off-shore deepwater marks wait for the adventurous angler visiting the Scottish islands. The Hebrides, Orkney and Shetland offer solitude and warm hospitality. The Channel Islands and Isle of Man, although quite near to the mainland, have a different ecology and undeniable off-shoreness when we look at their fishing.

Down toward the equator, sea angling takes on a big-game infuence. The Canary Islands, Madeira and the Azores boast the huge tunny, marlin and warm-water sharks. Fish with weird names like wahoo flash through the surface shoals of bait fish.

The Atlantic coasts of Spain and Portugal have a multitude of tiny ports where small boats can be hired to seek bass and blue fish. At the mouth of the Mediterranean Sea, we find the tiny colony of Gibraltar sitting amidst fine saltwater sport as the tunny, sharks and migratory bream pass through the Straits.

The roving sea angler, complete with caravan and all conveniences!

GLOSSARY

Backing Line wound on to the reel of a multiplier for sea fishing. When playing large fish, enormous compression forces are placed on the spool and the backing absorbs this.

Bale arm The revolving arm that winds line back on to the spool of a fixed-spool reel.

Bite An indication to the angler by sight, sound or touch that a fish has taken or mouthed the bait.

Bladderwrack Brown seaweed with wavy-edged fronds.

Blank A solid or hollow fibreglass tube from which rods are made.

Blenny One of a large family of small fishes living in shallow water.

Bomb A bomb-shaped lead with a swivel attached to the small end.

Breaking strain (b.s.) The test pull on fishing line measured in lb or kg when it breaks in the dry state.

Browse Midwater groundbait thrown in to attract fish such as mullet.

Casting Throwing out line by using the flexibility of the rod.

Centrepin reel A reel with the spool releasing line parallel to the rod.

Chum Small pieces of baitfish thrown into the water to attract fish.

Clutch Device allowing the spool of a reel to be disengaged; also a device that allows fish to take line to avoid breakage.

Cocktail Different baits on one hook, e.g. lugworm and squid.

Crimping Securing accessories on to rigs by squeezing metal ferrules round the line with a crimper.

Cuddy Collapsible shelter on a small boat.

Dan buoy A flag-topped floating marker buoy attached to a weight on the seabed. Used to pin-point a known fishing mark.

Deadbaiting Fishing with dead fish as bait for predatory species.

Demersal zone The part of the sea on and near the bottom.

Dinghy A small boat powered by oars or an outboard motor.

Drag Unnatural movement of line on the surface of the water. Or, a slipping clutch on fixed-spool reels and multipliers.

Drum A spool round which line is wound.

Dustbin The well-known beach-casting mark at Dungeness, Kent, where shore anglers can cast into deep water.

Echo sounder Electronic device that measures the depth below the boat and which can also produce a profile of the seabed below the boat.

Fathom A nautical measurement of 6 ft (1.8 m).

Fixed-spool reel A reel which has the spool at right angles to the rod. A revolving arm picks line up and winds it round the spool or drum.

Flatfish Fish that begin life in the upright position, but before maturity one eye travels round the top of the head to join the other. The fish then swims along the sea floor on one side of its body.

Flattie, *see* Flatfish.

Float fishing Using a float to register bites from taking fish.

Fry Immature fish.

Gaff Pole mounted with a hook to lift heavy fish from the water.

Gear ratio The difference between one turn of the reel handle and the number of turns of the spool.

Goby A group of small fishes, with about ten species in the North Atlantic.

Grapnel A multi-pronged anchor-like instrument used to hold boats over a rough, stony seabed.

Grip lead A weight with wires or protrusions designed to hold it still on the bottom while a tide is running.

Kelp Long, tough brown seaweeds that are attached to the seabed.

Lash (or lask) Thick slice of flesh from the side of a baitfish.

Lateral line A line of connected cells running down both flanks of a fish. They form part of the sensory system, enabling the fish to position itself in relation to its environment.

Littoral zone The sea shore, the area between high and low-water marks.

Lead Weight used to cock floats or as leger sinkers.

Layback method A style of shore/beach casting devised by Leslie Moncrieff.

Lure Any artificial bait.

Mark A known area or position where fish are to be found.

Multiplier A centre-pin reel with a gearing to turn the spool more times than a single turn of the reel handle.

Overrun Knotted bunch of line on the drum of a multiplier caused by lack of control while casting.

Party boat Craft manned by professional boatmen taking chartered parties out fishing.

Paternoster Terminal tackle with the lead at the bottom and the hooks above on booms.

Peeler The state of a crab when it has shed its shell and the replacement is still soft.

Pelagic zone The surface part of the open sea, or ocean.

Pirk An artificial lure with enough weight to be used without additional lead.

Ratchet A device on a reel that gives a clicking sound when line is being pulled off the spool by a fish.

Redgill A rubber or plastic lure that represents a sandeel.

Rig The terminal tackle ending with the baited hook.

Rings Guides that carry the line and spread the load along the rod.

Rotten bottom Line of weaker b.s. than the reel line, used to attach the weights to the rig. If snagged, the rotten bottom breaks and allows the angler to recover expensive terminal tackle.

Round fish Species such as the cod family, sea basses, etc, other than the flatfishes (which see).

Rubby dubby A nauseous concoction of old fish, offal, pilchard oil, that is released from a shark boat. Its odour stream is detected by the shark, which follow it up to the baited hooks.

Sandbar Barrier formed at the head of estuaries. A hazard to large boats but can be good fishing grounds.

Sea wrack Brown and red seaweeds often thrown up on shore after a storm.

Shock leader Line of stronger b.s. than the reel line, used to take the strain during casting heavy leads.

Terminal tackle Simple or complex system of hooks, swivels, snoods, traces attached to the reel line.

Test curve The pull on line that brings it to a right angle with the rod. Used to determine the balanced b.s. for the rod.

Tilley lamp Paraffin pressure lamp used by night-time beach anglers.

INDEX

Page numbers in **bold** refer to main entries
Page numbers in *italics* refer to illustrations

ACKNOWLEDGEMENTS

Dr Dietrich Burkel for the illustrations of the marine fishes of the North Atlantic.

Chris Jones for the tackle and technical illustrations.

Trevor King, of Dubery's Fishing Tackle, Hornchurch, Essex, for his many kindnesses and never failing good humour.

Mrs. Debbie Prichard for her preparation of the manuscript.

Mustad for the hook illustrations on pages 48, 49 and 51, and Lowrance for their echo sounder working drawings on pages 21 and 23.

All those sea anglers who have helped me and imparted, so freely, of their experience over the years.

Len Cacutt for copy editing and advice.

Caroline Hill – art editor and cover designer.

Goodwin Dorman – design.

Robin L.K. Wood – editor.